Alastair Sawday's

Special
places to stay

GARDEN BED & BREAKFAST

Typesetting, Conversion & Repro:...... Avonset, Bath

Maps:... Maps in Minutes, Cornwall

Printing:.. Midas Book Printers, UK

Design:.. Patrick Harrison, Caroline King
& Springboard Design, Bristol

UK Distribution:............................... Portfolio, Greenford, Middlesex

US Distribution:............................... The Globe Pequot Press,
Guilford, Connecticut

Published in November 2000

Alastair Sawday Publishing Co. Ltd
The Home Farm, Barrow Gurney, Bristol BS48 3RW

The Globe Pequot Press
P. O. Box 480
Guilford, Connecticut 06437
USA

First edition 2000

A catalogue record for this book is available from the British Library.

Alastair Sawday has asserted his right to be identified as the author of this work.

ISBN 1-901970-14-0 in the UK

ISBN 0-7627-0772-0 in the US

Printed in Slovenia

The publishers have made every effort to ensure the accuracy of the information in the book at the time of going to press. However, they cannot accept any responsibility for any loss, injury or inconvenience resulting from the use of information contained in this guide.

Alastair Sawday's

Special
places to stay

Garden Bed & Breakfast

"It is only to the gardener that time is a friend,
giving each year more than he steals."

Beverley Nichols

Guilford
Connecticut, USA

Alastair Sawday Publishing
Bristol, UK

Contents

Contents

Acknowledgements

For years we have pitched our editors/researchers into the deep end, largely out of habit. But James really took a major plunge when we asked him to do this book in winter - the height of the garden season, of course. Hardly a soul dared to show him a garden until the spring had worked its magic, so the poor fellow was much delayed. But the final result of all the frustration is a splendid book, in which James writes with masssive enthusiasm about other people's enthusiasms.

Driving the project along has been Jackie King, the Managing Editor of our British books. She has the patience of a hardy perennial and the book would never have blossomed without her. When James needed help with the database Kate Harris offered it and has dug away stoically for months, handling huge chunks of the administration as well. The book owes much to her. Julia Richardson has co-ordinated a complex production project with her usual panache and doggedness, bringing it all together in a last flourish of speed and skill. Jayne Warren has lent us her PR skills and loyal support, while Patrick Harrison has worked hard on the design front to make the book such a joy to look at.

Perhaps the biggest tribute should go to the gardeners whose passions and sheer hard work have made this book possible. We admire them and want you to do so, too.

Alastair Sawday

Series Editor:.. Alastair Sawday

Writer & researcher:.. James Belsey

Managing Editor:.. Jackie King

Production Manager:... Julia Richardson

Administration:.. Kate Harris

Accounts:... Bridget Bishop

All things web:.. Russell Wilkinson

PR/Marketing:.. Jayne Warren

Symbols:.. Mark Brierley

Introduction

How tantalising it is to walk past a garden and have to peer surreptitiously over the hedge for little more than a glimpse, and to walk furtively past a beautiful house pretending not to look inside. The solution is to buy this book, for with it you can get inside both garden and house - legitimately!

We cannot claim to be the first with this idea - there is a splendid booklet called *B&B for Garden Lovers* - but we were keen to publish a book in our own style, with colour photographs. We also wanted to shout a little more loudly about the extraordinary places (many of which also feature in our B&B book) which offer you such a remarkable combination of pleasures.

I am slightly humbled by George Mikes, who wrote *How To Be An Englishman*, and who said "You must not praise the elegance of an Englishman's house - though you may always be impressed by the garden." Here I am putting my name to a book which does both, and does it for the Welsh and the Scots, too.

Not only that, but I write this introduction with a touch of coyness. I may be known for my strong views on many things and even for my activities in defence of the undefendable (such as green-field sites awaiting the bulldozer), but I am less known for my knowledge of garden matters. Indeed, the following says it: "My garden will not make me famous/ I am a horticultural ignoramus." However, I have solved that one by getting James Belsey to select and write about these glorious gardens and the owners to approve what we say. The result is fascinating.

So, if you want to be allowed to wander around someone else's glorious acres and to swap stories of plantings, cuttings and prunings with fellow gardeners; if you want new ideas and to revel in the Herculean horticultural labours of others; if you want to lie back on the lawn after breakfast and a night to remember and admire some wondrous creations, then this book is for you. It is a worthy addition to our *Special Places* series. In fact, if you have all three of our UK books you will now have the rarest and most remarkable bunch of places to sleep in, and friends to make.

Alastair Sawday

Introduction

How do we choose our Special Places?

It's simple really; we just look for houses and owners that we like. Our approach has always been different from everybody else's. We ignore the rating systems used by most other publishers and our selection criteria are purely subjective. This can get us into trouble with owners, for it is hard to explain such personal decisions, but it has worked brilliantly because we can be ourselves and include some wonderful places and people that would slip through other nets.

The 'stars' and 'diamonds' used by other guides and by tourist boards are, we feel, fairly meaningless; we look for impressive architecture, settings that make us swoon, owners who exude generosity and kindness. We look, too, for natural comfort and an easy atmosphere. The things we seek cannot be measured. The homogenous, the corporate, the predictable are always rejected.

Now, after 23 books, we know that we have been hitting the right buttons. Our books are hugely popular and have - even more satisfyingly - become trusted. (This is in spite of the fact that we ask owners to pay a fee; we need to, for these are enormously admin-heavy projects, and colour books are expensive.)

We have applied the same selection criteria to this book, our first guide to Garden Bed & Breakfast in Britain. This is an extra-special guide, too, for you will not only be given memorable bed and breakfast but you will be staying with knowledgeable garden-lovers whose creativity has been put to work both inside and outside the house.

Whether they have a town courtyard or stately parkland, what matters is that they are passionate about collecting, planting and nurturing trees, shrubs, flowers, even wildflower meadows. They have all taken pride in weaving tapestries of colour and texture and shaping their gardens into places where they love to be. If you enjoy beautiful surroundings, you can't fail to be delighted, even if you can't tell a geranium from a jeroboam.

Here you'll find professional garden designers, award-winning gardens, gardens that are open for charity or for National Gardens Scheme days, plant nurseries and owners who organise gardens tours. They are people who will nurture your own enthusiasm for gardening (i.e. they will never make you feel inadequate!).

What to expect

The atmosphere in the houses will vary hugely and you'll find traditional country homes where you'll be expected to follow certain protocols, such as

Introduction

dressing for dinner, and you'll find the informal - maybe a farmhouse where guests, children, cats and dogs all come and go as they please.

Owners will differ, too, in how 'hands-on' they are - some will want to sit down with you for afternoon tea and chat, others will welcome you and then leave you to your own devices.

Whatever their style, all of our owners will make you feel spoiled - whether it be spending time showing you their garden, cooking you a magnificent breakfast, giving you everything you could possibly want for a comfortable night's sleep, or passing on their local knowledge.

These people are not slick hotel owners and, just as your own home-life can spring surprises, so can theirs. You'll meet real people in real homes - with families, pets, gardens and sometimes, even, other jobs to juggle - and there may be days when things don't go as smoothly as they would hope. You may be there on the day that the budgie dies and, thus, breakfast won't be served with the usual gusto. Equally, you may be there on the day of a family celebration and be swept into the fun. Unpredictability can work in your favour, too.

If you're not happy about something, it's better for everyone if you say so at the time. Most things can easily be put right, without fuss or embarrassment. Humour and politeness go a long way.

Many of our houses are sumptuous and luxurious, with owners willing to dance attendance on you, but it wouldn't be fair to treat them as hotels. Thus, it would be kind of you to make your bed if you are staying more than one night, to ask the owner if you may sit in the garden after breakfast, to tell them if you expect to be back very late. These issues will rarely pose a problem.

Finding the right place for you

We give honest descriptions of our houses, owners and gardens and hope that if you read them carefully you will end up in a place that suits you. You should certainly be able to glean how formal or informal a house is and the type of garden to expect. You might yearn to visit someone's romantic wild garden in a moorland setting, a whacky garden in central London or the elegance of a formal country house garden created around an historic home. It has been our aim to guide you to a house and garden from which you can draw inspiration.

Many hosts will be delighted to show you around their garden, but don't expect this as a duty. If times are busy they may well be unable to give you a guided tour. If you admire certain plants, most passionate gardeners are

Introduction

only too happy to take a cutting for you, but that is their gift and not an obligation. To take a cutting without permission (i.e. pinch it) is not good gardening etiquette!

At the back of the book you will find our quick-reference indices. These are a county-by-county guide to houses which use mostly organic or home-grown, chemical-free produce, have ground-floor bedrooms and bathrooms for those with limited mobility, have full facilities for wheelchair users and are good for single people (have single rooms or charge no single supplement).

How to use this book

We strive to make our books user-friendly. We hope that we have succeeded - readers like the clear maps, the easy-to-use indices and the layouts. Do tell us if you have any ideas for improvement.

Maps

When you know which part of Britain you want to stay in, look at the map at the front of the book, find your area and look for the nearest houses. Don't focus on the county headings throughout the book as you could discount ideal solutions - the perfect B&B to stay in after the Suffolk wedding might lie just over the border, in Norfolk or Essex.

Types of Properties

There is a huge difference in the luxuriousness of our *Special Places*. The price can be an indicator of how lavish your surroundings will be, but we expect you to find good value in each of them.

There is a huge variety, too, in the size and grandness of the gardens. The emphasis is on people who love their gardens, so although we may have found a small plot or a developing garden, the owner's enthusiasm carries it off. We delight as much in the tiny town container garden or the simple cottagey plot as in the stately and the formal. We are sure that you will, too. Many owners are modest about what they have and what they have created, charmingly but unnecessarily so.

Do consider the position of the house when making your choice. If, for instance, traffic noise bothers you, check on the map and consult the directions for any sign of nearby busy roads or railways. If you are travelling with children, you may prefer the space of a farmhouse rather than a tiny cottage where you'll be cheek-by-jowl with other guests.

Beds and Bathrooms

We state if rooms are double/twin/single. Many are large enough to take

Introduction

a foldaway bed for a child, so do ask when booking if this is possible and what the charge will be.

The description of bathroom details varies and owners prefer you to discuss your preferences on the phone. It may be possible, for instance, to have sole use of a 'shared' bathroom if that matters very much to you.

'En suite' means 'attached'...i.e. it is yours, off the bedroom.

'Private' means that the room is not en suite but for your sole use - perhaps across the corridor.

'Shared' means that you will be sharing either with other guests or family members.

Other Rooms

In most houses you will share sitting areas with the family; in a few there are private sitting rooms for guests. If this is an important subject for you, make sure that you know what to expect before you arrive. A few houses have no sitting room for guests - some of these will have large bedrooms with armchairs or sofas.

Prices

We have stated the price per person sharing a room and including full English breakfast, unless otherwise stated.

Single people: if there is no single room, we often give a price for one person's use of a double room (single occupancy). If none is mentioned, it is still worth discussing on the phone.

This is a biennial book that lasts until 2002; during that time owners will put up their prices, so do confirm on the phone what you will pay.

Symbols

We have a checklist at the front of the book. The symbols are not an unequivocal statement of fact - use them as a guide and a point from which to begin your discussions with owners. If an owner has a 'Pets Welcome' symbol, tell her about your dog/parrot so that she can consider the other guests and make a decision.

Equally, if an owner doesn't have a symbol that you are looking for, it is worth discussing your needs. It may be that a hostess who doesn't have a 'Children Welcome' symbol may be willing to accommodate your little ones if she has no other guests.

Introduction

Practical Matters

Meals

We have stated if the owner provides packed lunch/lunch/supper/dinner for guests and the price per person. Most hosts are happy to cook for you with advance warning, thus the 'by arrangement' stipulation.

Tell your host of any dietary requirements - most are imaginative, competent cooks and like to use the freshest local ingredients and garden produce.

If you are travelling a long way and, may arrive too late or too tired to venture out for supper, do ask owners if they can prepare something simple for you - even those who don't usually offer evening meals may be happy to help.

Ask your hosts for local recommendations if they do not do food. Say how far you'll be prepared to drive and give some indication of budget.

If the house is not licensed, and you are eating in, do take your own wine which your host will open/chill for you.

Seasons and Public Holidays

Bank holidays are the busiest times for our owners, so book early - especially if you want to have a particular room.

With gardens in mind, April to September are, of course, the months to see them in fullest bloom and these are the most popular months for visiting Britain's well-known gardens, too (see our guide at the back of the book). Certainly during these times, you can expect your host to be spending many daylight hours in the garden and public gardens to be busy.

Bookings

Hosts will take bookings by phone, post, fax or e-mail, although most prefer the former so that you can get a feel for each other. If your arrangements are complicated, it is best to confirm them in writing to ensure that you get the right combination of bathrooms and bedrooms, or that dietary needs are met.

Do let your host know roughly what time you will arrive and call if you are delayed. Most will want to be there when you arrive and to spend some time with you. If you have booked an evening meal, do be prompt.

Owners vary in their preferred arrival and departure times; we like to hear of relaxed, rather than rigid, rules. If you feel you are being asked to arrive unreasonably late and leave unreasonably early, do let us know.

Introduction

It can be hard to drag yourself away after a full breakfast, so if you would like to read the paper in the garden, just ask. If you would like to drop off your bags mid-afternoon before setting off on a walk, again the owner is unlikely to mind.

Deposits and Cancellations

Many owners will ask for a deposit - the size varies enormously. If you have to cancel and the room cannot be re-let, your deposit will often not be refunded.

We do not have a policy on deposits and cancellations - it is impossible to design a contract that covers all eventualities and we do not meddle in the WAY in which our owners run their houses. We do regard a booking as an informal contract between host and guest and advise that the cancellation policy should be discussed at the time of booking.

Payment

Most houses do not accept credit card payments. Those that do will have a 'Credit Card' symbol. Others will accept cash or cheques.

Children

Owners that accept children of any age have a 'Children Welcome' symbol. Those who accept children of certain ages do not have a symbol but a line printed at the end of their house description - *Children over eight welcome*, for example.

Many owners love children, even if they don't have the symbol, but don't want to advertise the fact for fear of putting off couples travelling without children. They therefore keep quiet about their climbing frames, lest they portray their elegant retreat as some sort of crèche.

Even in those houses that do have the child symbol, you should try to control the uncontrollable. One man's adored infant is another man's caterwauling horror.

Safety is a subject high in the minds of many of the owners in these books. Lakes, ponds, water features, mills, streams and rivers make some gardens dangerous for unaccompanied children. The 'Child Welcome' symbol doesn't mean 'Child Safe'.

Dogs

Do dogs and special gardens mix? They can and some of the less formal houses would no more turn away your furry friend than they would you. Some of these houses will accept well-behaved dogs, but you must be

Introduction

honest about your pet - are they likely to chase the ducks/jump in the fountain/dig holes? Do chat to your host beforehand.

Smoking

The 'No-Smoking' symbol means no smoking anywhere in the house. The absence of the symbol doesn't mean that you may light up anywhere, it means that you should ask the owner where you may smoke. You should, of course, be sensitive to other guests.

Tipping

Owners do not expect you to tip them. If you have encountered extraordinary kindness, you may like to leave a little gift or to send a 'thank you' card. It is rewarding for owners if you write to tell us of your good fortune (we record all feedback from readers).

Environment

We seek to reduce our impact on the environment where possible by:

- Planting trees to compensate for our carbon emissions (as calculated by Edinburgh University); we are officially a carbon-neutral publishing company.

- Re-using paper, recycling stationery, tins, bottles, etc.

- Encouraging staff use of bicycles (they're given free) and encouraging car-sharing.

- Celebrating the use of organic, home and locally-produced food.

- Publishing books that support, in however small a way, the rural economy and small-scale businesses.

- Encouraging our owners to follow recommendations made to them by the Energy Efficiency Centre to make their homes more environmentally friendly.

Subscriptions

Owners pay to appear in this guide, their fee goes towards the high production costs of an all-colour book.

We only include places and owners that we find special. It is not possible for anyone to buy their way in.

Introduction

Disclaimer

We make no claims to pure objectivity in judging our *Special Places to Stay*. They are here because we like them. Our opinions and tastes are ours alone and this book is a statement of them; we hope that you will share them.

We have done our utmost to get our facts right but apologise unreservedly for any mistakes that may have crept in. Sometimes, too, prices shift, usually upwards and 'things' change. We should be grateful to be told of any errors or changes, however small.

Special Places to Stay on the Internet

By the time you read this we will have roughly a thousand entries on the online database which is our web site www.sawdays.co.uk. These are from the various titles in the *Special Places to Stay* series so, if you like the places in this book, why not browse some more?

We flatter ourselves that the 8,000 visitors a month who come to the site have good reason to, and we think you should join them! It gives access to hundreds of places to stay across Europe and you can buy all our books direct through our window on the world wide web.

And Finally

We are thrilled to bring you this eclectic selection of houses, gardens and owners and urge you to discover their magic for yourselves. When you've put this unique guide to Garden Bed & Breakfast to the test, we would love to hear how you got on; feedback is vital to the success of each of our books. There is a report form at the back of the book, or you can e-mail us: specialplaces@sawdays.co.uk.

Remember that our highly successful British Bed & Breakfast book contains many more special B&Bs - lots of them with lovely gardens. Europe-wide, we have over 2,600 Special Places in Britain, Ireland, France, Spain, Portugal and Italy.

Many of the owners that feature in this new book had to be gently persuaded that their very own little corner of Britain was worthy of inclusion - we have included them because their gardens ARE special; nothing will encourage or delight them more than to welcome appreciative, garden-loving guests.

A short history of the company

Perhaps the best clue as to why these books have their own very particular style and 'bent' lies in Alastair's history.

After a law degree, a stint as a teacher in Voluntary Service Overseas led to a change in direction. He became a teacher (French and Spanish) and then a refugee worker, then spent several years in overseas development work before settling into environmental campaigning, and even green politics. Meanwhile, he was able to dabble - just once a year - in an old interest, taking clients on tours of special places all over Europe. This grew, eventually, into a travel company (it still exists as Alastair Sawday's Tours, operating, inter alia, walking and biking tours all over Europe).

Trying to take his clients to eat and sleep in places that were not owned by corporations and assorted bandits he found dozens of very special places in France - farms, châteaux etc - a list that grew into the first book, *French Bed and Breakfast*. It was a celebration of 'real' places to stay and the remarkable people who run them.

So, this publishing company is based on the success of that first and rather whimsical French book. It started as mild crusade, and there it stays. For we still celebrate the unusual, the beautiful, the highly individual. We have no rules for owners; they do things their own way. We are passionate about rejecting the ugly, the cold, the banal and the indifferent. And we are still passionate about promoting the use of 'real' food. Alastair is a trustee of the Soil Association and keen to promote organic growing especially.

It is a source of huge pleasure to us that we seem to have pressed the right button: there are thousands and thousands of people who, clearly, share our views and take up our ideas. We are by no means alone in trumpeting the virtues of standing up to the monstrous uniformity of so much of our culture.

The greatest accolade we have had was in *The Bookseller* magazine, which described us as 'head and shoulders above the rest'. That meant a lot. But even more satisfying is that we are building a company in which people matter. We are delighted to hear of new friendships between those in the book and those using it and to know that there are many people - among them artists, farmers, champions of the countryside - who have been enabled to pursue their unusual lives thanks to the extra income the book brings them.

Of course we want the company to flourish, but this isn't just about money; it is about people, too.

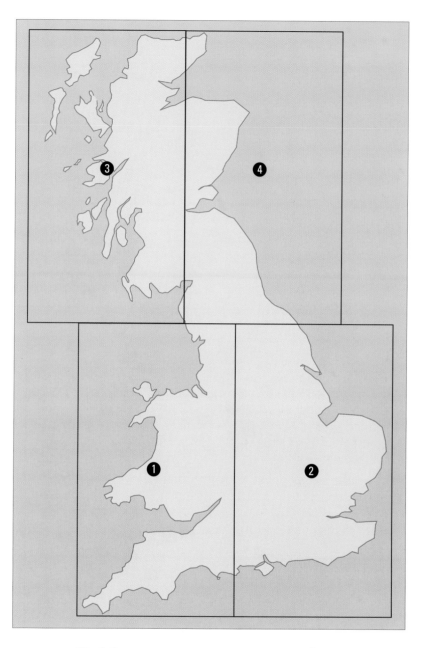

Guide to our map page numbers

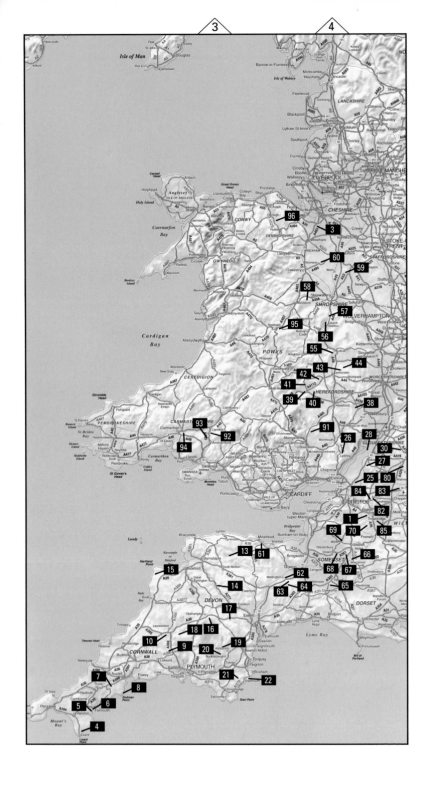

Map 1

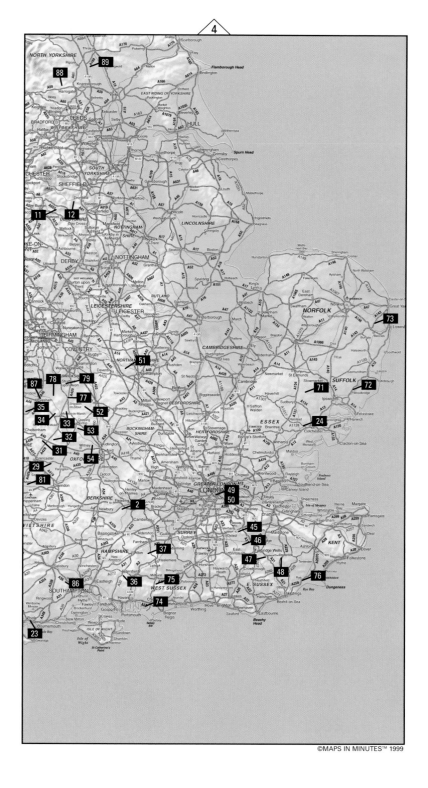

Map 2

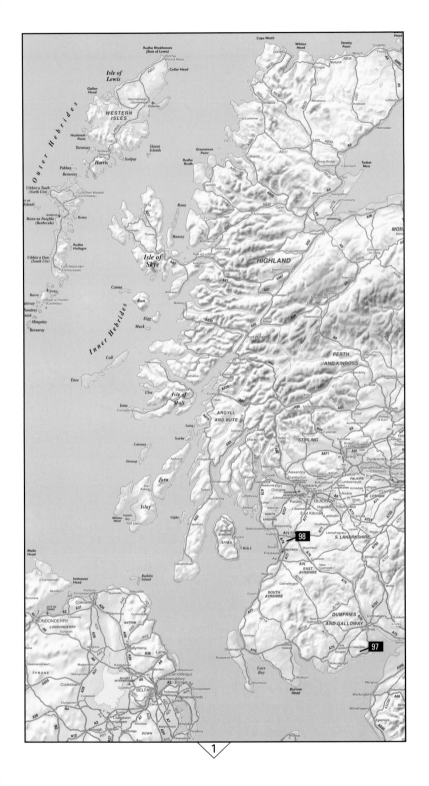

Map 3

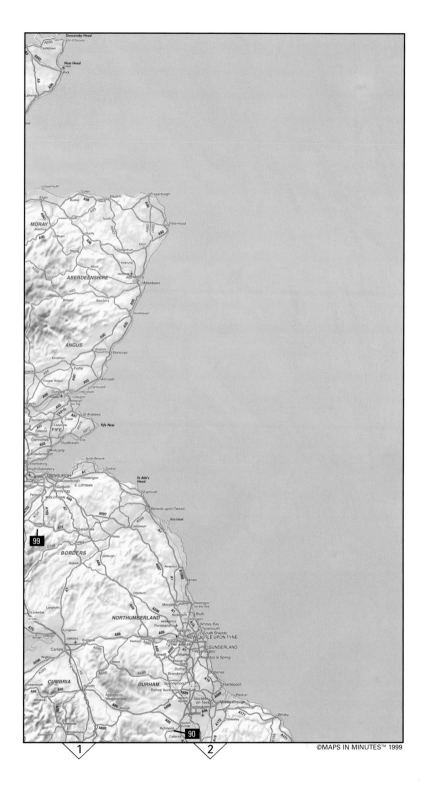

Map 4

England

AN ENCYCLOPAEDIC KNOWLEDGE OF PLANTS and a collector's delight in finding new treasures have unspired Jane and Anthony's south-west facing terraced garden. The main structure was laid out when the house was built in the 1860s, and their most cherished inheritance, a magnificent Robinia Pseudacia, was probably planted then. For 32 years they have been adding to the garden's attractions, planting the series of borders with labour-saving in mind, since they do most of the work themselves. It's a garden that's great fun to explore because of its sloping lay-out and secret paths. The large lawn at the upper level leads to another – and another. A vine planted on the main terrace wall in 1973 now covers 14 yards of wall in three tiers and a fan-trained apricot nestles beside it. Jane caught the climbing rose bug some years ago, hence the very large Paul's Himalayan Musk. There are more than 70 old roses and it is obvious that plants with scented leaves and flowers are much loved. The soil is free-draining alkaline, so sun lovers like cistus, hebe, euphorbias and phormiums have been chosen for the more open areas. Play boules or soak up the sun and scents on the main lawn, chat to your hosts about special plants, discover botanical treasures. A true garden-lover's garden with interesting plants to enjoy in every season.

Map No: 1

Grey Lodge

Summer Lane, Combe Down, Bath
Bath & N.E. Somerset BA2 7EU

Tel: 01225 832069 Fax: 01225 830161
greylodge@freenet.co.uk
www.sawdays.co.uk

Jane & Anthony Stickland

Combe Down is the landscape equivalent of Bath's Royal Crescent – stunning. Bath stone was discovered here (by Ralph Allen, who consequently made his fortune) and trundled down the hill to build all that celebrated Regency elegance. Staggering views across the hilly Somerset landscape – the Sticklands have even installed a full-height window to take it all in. Breakfasts, with organic eggs and 'proper' bacon, are a real treat. Fluffy towels, herb, fruit and flower teas in your room. A warm, kind and likeable couple.

Rooms:
2 twins/doubles and 1 family room,
all en suite (shower).
Price:
From £30 p.p. Single supp. £5.
£5 supp. per room for one-night booking.
Meals:
Dinner, 3 courses, £16 p.p.
4 courses, £18 p.p. B.Y.O. wine.
Closed:
Christmas.

From A36 about 3 miles out of Bath on the Warminster road, take uphill road by traffic lights and Viaduct Inn. Take 1st turn left, signed Monkton Combe. After village (0.5 miles on) Grey Lodge is first house on left.

A YOUNG, DEVELOPING GARDEN with 10 acres which are being transformed into a mix of the formal and informal, and views across open farmland in a deeply rural corner of Berkshire. One gorgeous feature is already in place: a beautifully worked, elaborate knot garden in the form of two roses, its little box hedges set among pristine gravel. Another is a long pergola heavy with roses and honeysuckle. There are as many family associations in the garden as there are inside Peter and Rosemary's home. One is the eye-catching stately sorbus avenue which was planted to celebrate their daughter's wedding; edged by tall, waving, uncut grasses, it leads you to a shady, creeper-covered bower with countryside beyond. Roses clamber up the façade of the house and the wide, open, sunny patio guarded by two bay sentinels in containers is a lovely place to sit and enjoy the view while a fountain splashes. An intimate side patio is bounded by flowers and hedges, with an arch covered in golden hop and honeysuckle. Deer abound, so Rosemary chooses plants which they dislike! Specimen trees are being planted across the 10 acres and, beyond the tall enclosing hedge sheltering the large croquet lawn, an avenue of ancient oaks bears witness to the centuries-old history of the manor. A handsome garden in the making and one which grows with interest all the time.

Rooms:
2 doubles, both en suite.
Price:
£35 p.p. £50 single occ.
Meals:
Supper, 3 courses, with wine, £12.50 p.p.
Closed:
Christmas & New Year.

From junction 12 on M4 towards Newbury. Follow signs to Theale station, go over railway to traffic lights. 500 yds on, turn right. Keep on country road for 0.75 miles, then left at x-roads. House entrance straight ahead.

Time-travel through the friendly Rosemary and Peter's luxurious house, part 1600s manor, part 1950s, part 1990s. The drawing room, with deep sofas, is modern and the cosy breakfast room is beamed. Bedrooms, one with a four-poster, are in the old part of the manor, with beamed ceilings and every comfort – one has a whirlpool bath. Family pictures give a homely touch and guests are treated as friends. Delicious dinners – both Rosemary and Peter are excellent cooks – are served at the long dining table sparkling with silver. Prepare to be pampered.

The Old Manor

Whitehouse Green, Sulhamstead, Reading, Berkshire RG7 4EA

Tel: 0118 983 2423   Fax: 0118 983 6262

Rosemary & Peter Sanders-Rose

The Mount

Higher Kinnerton, Chester, Cheshire CH4 9BQ

Tel: 01244 660275   Fax: 01244 660275

Jonathan & Rachel Major

"Our guests seem to oversleep". This is peace indeed. A haven for garden buffs, walkers, birdwatchers – Britain at its best with a fruitful kitchen garden, scented conservatory, a tennis court and a genuine welcome from Rachel. She also embroiders her own designs which can be seen around the house. It is furnished in elegant, traditional style and the proportions of the light-filled drawing room and the big, high-ceilinged dining room feel just right. The bedrooms are light and large and your hosts like to treat their visitors as guests of the family.

Map No: 1

A HAVEN FOR GARDEN BUFFS and birdwatchers – you might catch sight of careering young sparrowhawks testing their wings overhead. The collection of old and very beautiful trees dates back to the building of the house in 1860 while the garden's three-acre outline was set out in the early 1950s. Rachel has worked wonders with grounds which were once simply open lawns and trees, with new projects constantly under way. The mood everywhere is informal and the garden has developed gradually and naturally over the years, reflecting Rachel and Jonathan's growing interest and commitment to gardening. The front garden's croquet lawn, overlooked by trees, takes you down steps past stone pineapples into the cool seclusion of woodland, with huge Paul's Himalayan Musk and Francis E Lester roses soaring dizzily up a tall conifer. Roses, clematis and hydrangea sparkle on The Mount's façade as house-martins flit in and out of nests beneath the eaves. One of Rachel's recent additions is a pond to one side of the house – a mass of bulrushes, foxgloves and iris that is a haven for wildlife. The mood behind the house is more open and free, its grandness decorated with new beech hedges to give shape and form. The handsome pergola is clad in wisteria underplanted with lavender, a charming combination. A newly-planted arbour of willows leads to a bountifully planted herbaceous border brimming with colour. A lovely garden in perfect harmony with the handsome Victorian house.

Rooms:
1 double and 1 twin/double, both en suite (bath); 1 twin, en suite (shower).
Price:
From £24 p.p.
Meals:
Good village pubs within walking distance.
Closed:
Christmas week-3 January.

From Chester, A55 west, then A5104 to Broughton. Left at roundabout to Pennyffordd on A5104. Through Broughton & over A55. First left to Kinnerton down Lesters Lane. House on right.

THE POSITION IS SIMPLY STUNNING and Marion and Peter have gardened assiduously to complement the garden's glorious outlook. This is Cornwall at its mildest and Marion has taken much inspiration from the exotic gardens at Tresco. It's a few degrees cooler than the Scilly Isles, a helicopter flight away, so Marion can't use the full palette Tresco employs, but nonetheless you will be green with envy. The lushness and range of tender plants which thrive wonderfully in these carefully nurtured, delightfully informal grounds is impressive. When they moved here, they completed the restoration of their delightful home before turning their full attention to their two acres. They inherited mature trees and drystone walls, but the hard landscaping which gives this garden its shape and layout is their creation. Opposite the front door you'll find Cornwall-loving camellias and rhododendrons underplanted by masses of spring flowers, with a row of box 'soldiers' standing to attention on the path. Rosarians will love the rose garden edged by lavender and a pretty hedge of the miniature rose Ballerina. Below the tall garden wall is a deep border packed with colour and interest and, near the house, a stunning 'hot' garden of spiky architectural plants with dramatic foliage. Informal, lived-in... and with wonderful details like the lichens softening bark and tree trunks.

Rooms:
1 four-poster, 1 half-tester,
1 twin/double, all en suite
(bath/shower).
Price:
£39-£46 p.p. Single supp. £10.
Meals:
Dinner, 3 courses, £22.95 p.p.,
by arrangement.
Closed:
Christmas.

From Helston, A3083 south. Just before Lizard, left to Church Cove. Follow signs for about 0.75 miles. House on left behind blue gates.

The view of garden to church to sea to headland is heart-stopping and the ever-changing light casts a spell over the landscape. The dining room is illuminated by fire and candle; the yellow drawing room, with wooden floors and deep sofas, is perfect. Cascading drapes, immaculate linen, a regal four-poster and a luxurious half-tester – the bedrooms are exquisite. Marion speaks with passion and humour of her piece of England. Swim in the sheltered, heated pool or breathe deeply of clean Cornish air while walking the three minutes to the sea. Irresistible.

Map No: 1

Landewednack House

Church Cove, The Lizard, Cornwall TR12 7PQ

Tel: 01326 290909   Fax: 01326 290192   landewednackhouse@virgin.uk

Peter & Marion Stanley

A TRULY SECRET GARDEN, utterly unexpected when you arrive at this ancient, stone-built manor house. You can tell that Judy and Mike are keen gardeners from the banked garden across the lane and from the front door with its bountiful planting. But it's when the latch lifts and the garden door set in the wall swings open that you get the real impact. Suddenly you're confronted by one garden, a peep into the second and a final view to the third along an eye-catching vista. The shape of these three areas is historic; this was a working farm until 1919 and the further areas were holding pens for cattle. The garden blends the formal with the informal and each of the three south-facing 'compartments' has a mood of its own; outdoor rooms are linked by granite archways, a tunnel-like herbaceous border and a rose garden edged by neat, low hedges. Gravelled paths tempt you to move from one area to the next, enjoying the carefully-worked displays. Lots of camellias in the early part of the year and plenty of semi-tropical plant life thanks to the mild conditions. A sunny croquet lawn, a well-tended kitchen garden where Mike grows the more unusual vegetables and a shady orchard complete the picture. Guests may also be allowed a peep at Judy's mother's garden next door – completely different and created from a sloping field. It's a mini gem of planting with a final crescendo of soaring gunnera at the foot of the slope.

Rooms:
1 twin with private bathroom;
2 doubles, both en suite (bath).
Price:
£23.50-£28.50 p.p. Single supp.
in high season, £12.
Meals:
Dinner, 4 courses, with wine £19 p.p.
Closed:
Christmas.

From Truro, take Falmouth road (A39). At Hillhead roundabout follow sign to Constantine. 0.5 miles after High Cross garage turn left to Port Navas. House is opposite the granite mushrooms.

Begun in the 13th century, 'modernised' in the 16th century, the house has sweeping views to open country and the distant Helford river. Country-house elegance entwined with a higgledy-piggledy lived-in feel: warm kitchen, lots of antiques, dark oak, open fireplace and a granite-walled, deep green, candlelit dining room. Bedrooms are cosy and stocked with good books, jugs of fresh water and home-made biscuits. Judy makes her own bread and preserves, too; both she and Mike are easy hosts.

Map No: 1

Treviades Barton

High Cross, Constantine, nr. Falmouth, Cornwall TR11 5RG

Tel: 01326 340524   Fax: 01326 340524
treviades.barton@btinternet.com   btinternet.com/~treviades.barton

Judy & Mike Ford

Carwinion

Mawnan Smith, nr. Falmouth, Cornwall TR11 5JA

Tel: 01326 250258   Fax: 01326 250903
jane@carwinion.freeserve.co.uk

Mr & Mrs Anthony Rogers

Map No: 1

If an inquisitive, errant dinosaur came rustling out of the great stands of bamboo or soaring gunnera, you honestly wouldn't be surprised. These 12 acres are a ravishing homage to leaf, foliage, wildness... a heavenly place of trees, ponds, streams. No wonder that Jane, who has done so much for these grounds in recent years, calls it an "unmanicured garden". At the end of the 19th century, Anthony's grandfather planted the first bamboos in this gorgeous valley garden leading down to the Helford river. Today Carwinion has one of the finest collections in Europe, more than 130 species with wonderful leaf and stem forms... the Bamboo Society of Great Britain flock here for annual get-togethers. The lushness soars impressively to the sky – don't miss the 20-foot Pieris. Jane has made a series of paths to lead you through one breathtakingly romantic area after another, a palm sheltering under a tall beech tree, a banana tree thriving in the mild atmosphere. Tree ferns soar and, in a final flourish at the foot of the garden, Jane has transformed an old quarry into an enchanting fern garden. Camellia lovers will be knocked out by the walled garden where the renowned camellia grower John Price has now established his Towan Camellias business, offering more than 300 varieties and 100 types of hydrangea. Magic everywhere.

Originally a small farmhouse built in 1790, this rambling manor was enlarged in the 1840s shortly after the garden was originally designed and planted. The manor has the faded grandeur and collections of oddities (corkscrews, penknives, magnifying glasses) that successive generations hand on. Your charmingly eccentric host will introduce you to his ancestors, his antiques, his fine big old bedrooms – and he and the tireless Jane serve "a breakfast to be reckoned with". The self-catering wing has a fenced garden to keep your children in and Carwinion dogs out.

Rooms:
1 double, 2 twins/doubles, both en suite (bath).
Price:
£30 p.p. Single supp. £5.
Self-catering £125-£275 per week.
Meals:
Available locally.
Dinner by arrangement.
Closed:
Never.

Take left road in Mawnam Smith at Red Lion pub, onto Carwinion Road. 400 yds up hill on right, sign for Carwinion Garden.

Creed House

Creed, Grampound, Truro, Cornwall TR2 4SL

Tel: 01872 530372

Lally & William Croggon

*In Lally and William's lovely house and garden there's a comforting
sense that all is well in England's green and pleasant land. St.
Crida's church rises on tip-toes above treetops while the murmur of a
lazy stream reaches your ears. Inside the 1730s house, shimmering
wooden floors are covered with Persian rugs and light pours into every
elegant corner. Breakfast at the mahogany table has a habit of
turning into an early morning house-party, such is Lally's sense of
fun and spontaneity. The big guestrooms exude taste and simplicity.
Children over eight welcome.*

HERE IS ONE OF CORNWALL'S LOVELIEST GARDENS, a tribute to the enormous amount of hard work, wonderful planting, dedication and brilliant plantsmanship devoted to these stunning seven acres of garden and woodland. Lally and William came here in 1974 to find a Miss Havisham of a garden with a lawn like a hayfield edged in brambles and the rest an impenetrable jungle with glimpses of 40-ft high rhododendrons, magnolia and huge stands of gunnera. There clearly had been a garden here once upon a time – they determined to restore and embellish it. Today this jungle has been transformed into a fine, gentle, old-fashioned rectory garden. Along the way they discovered many exciting buildings under the brambles including a strange cobbled yard with a sunken centre and a summer house which they have carefully restored. The mass clearance also encouraged long-dormant snowdrops and daffodils to bloom in their thousands within a year. The tree and shrub collection is outstanding; rhododendrons, camellias, azaleas and magnolias do brilliantly and secret paths leading from the gently sloping lawns lure you deep into the dappled delights of the decorative woodland. So much to admire and enjoy, such as the circular lily pond, the swamp garden with its candelabra primulas and mecanopsis and the lower stable yard with its alpines and sunloving plants on its raised wall beds. Do ask Lally and William to take you around the grounds. They're delightful, enthusiastic and very knowledgeable and their pleasure in their masterpiece is totally infectious.

Rooms:
3 twins/doubles:
1 en suite (bath/shower),
2 with private bathrooms.
Price:
£30-£35 p.p. Single supp.
by arrangement.
Meals:
Available locally.
Closed:
Christmas & New Year.

From St Austell, A390 to Grampound. Just beyond the clock tower, left into Creed Lane. After 1 mile left at grass triangle opposite church. House is behind 2nd white gate on left.

Bodrugan Barton

Mevagissey, Cornwall PL26 6PT

Tel: 01726 842094   Fax: 01726 844378
bodruganbarton@ukonline.co.uk   www.sawdays.co.uk

Sally & Tim Kendall

SALLY AND TIM'S FARMLAND GARDEN is set amid beautiful coastal scenery – part of the farm runs down to the sea with paths edged with sea pinks and other salt spray tolerant wild flowers. The mood is completely informal, blending in with the surrounding landscape. Around the house is a garden in the making, with a simple front lawn and border and, taking shape behind the house, a walled and hedged garden. Sally is determined to transform the land into something of beauty which she and her family and visitors can enjoy, either glimpsed from bedroom windows or as a place to wander or sit. Herculean efforts have included the back-breaking business of removing old concrete paths to create prettier and softer lines. There is a slated area just outside the kitchen window – dominated by a tall rambling rose climbing up the wall, and with large and small containers with hostas and a grand gunnera, it is an enclosed, intimate corner. Sally and Tim are carefully landscaping the area around the pool house, using pink and blue theming in the newly created banks above the patio which has an open air chess set. Wildflower areas beyond the garden are being developed and cherished and more than 350 trees have been planted. Come in late April and May and you'll be thrilled, not only by the garden, but by the masses of wild flowers that surround the coastal paths.

Sir Henry de Bodrugan lived here – he was a renowned host and, 500 years on, Tim and Sally uphold the tradition with sackfuls of enthusiasm. Everything's freshly decorated; there are family antiques, the promise of home-made bread and good food. In the dining room, even with sofas, woodburner and piano, you could turn a cartwheel. An ancient lane flanked by flowers leads you to Colona Bay: small, secluded and full of rock pools where Robin, their son, catches 'blennies' by hand. It's blissful. There's an indoor heated pool and sauna, too. Heligan and the Eden project are nearby. Children over 12 welcome.

Rooms:
1 double, en suite (shower); 1 double and 1 twin, both with private bathroom.
Price:
£25-£30 p.p.
Meals:
Dinner £12-£20 p.p.
Packed Lunch from £4 p.p.
Closed:
Christmas & New Year.

From St. Austell to Mevagissey. Through village, up steep hill and down into Portmellon. Up steep hill, left-hand bend, entrance is 100 yards on.

RICHARD SAYS, SELF-DEPRECATINGLY, that Bicton Mill deserves a mention for its national collection of weeds... but then one man's weeds are another man's wildflowers. Richard and Mariebel have made their large, river- and leat-bound garden a perfectly harmonised blend of the wild and the informal. The long, park-like, luxurious lawn with its pretty bridge is edged by mature trees and gently flowing water; sea trout linger and, if they're not careful, are skilfully caught by Richard, a keen game fisherman. Mariebel knows her plants and has added scores of delightful touches and displays, especially in the terraced garden above the house with its bountiful planting and summer flowers. Do explore this part of the grounds – you'll find fascinating carved stonework which hints at the ancient history of this secluded, utterly peaceful valley and added interest like the huge cider press near the front door that has been transformed into a raised bed. A hefty pergola groans with vigorous climbers like Kiftsgate; a Rambling Rector spirals up the hillside. Across the little lane good shrubs and trees have been planted to create a separate garden – a sort of introduction to the main event. Spring-time is particularly magical here, with bluebells giving hazy displays in wilder areas. Later, autumnal drifts of windflowers shimmer like flamingoes. Don't listen to a word Richard says about weeds... this is a place of beauty and he and Mariebel have done much to enhance the valley that they love.

Rooms:
1 double, en suite (shower);
1 double, private bathroom.
Price:
£25-£30 p.p. Single supp.
by arrangement.
Meals:
Dinner £18 p.p., by arrangement.
Closed:
Never.

On A388 Callington-Launceston, left at Kelly Bray (opposite garage) to Maders. 400 yds after Maders, left to Golberdon and left at crossroads. After 400 yards, right down unmarked lane. Mill 0.75 miles on, by bridge.

An old corn mill with the original water-wheel now in the kitchen and with views down the garden to the salmon/sea trout river from the bedrooms. Richard is a keen fly fisherman and can fix up rods for visitors. Mariebel is a professional portrait painter who taught for many years; she's still happy to teach individuals or groups. Bicton is informal, comfortable and relaxed. Meals are eaten in the huge farmhouse kitchen or in the impressive slate-floored dining room. The Lynher Valley is unspoilt and enchanting, with lovely walks all round. Children by arrangement.

Bicton Mill

Bicton, nr. Liskeard, Cornwall PL14 5RF

Tel: 01579 383577   Fax: 01579 383577

Richard & Mariebel Allerton

Hornacott

South Petherwin, Launceston, Cornwall PL15 7LH

Tel: 01566 782461   Fax: 01566 782461

Jos & Mary-Anne Otway-Ruthven

A DYNAMIC GARDEN WHERE LOTS has been happening in recent years as Jos and Mary-Anne work their way from one area to the next. The garden is about one and a half acres of sloping ground with shady spots, open, sunny lawns and borders and many shrubs. A stream tumbles through the garden after heavy rain and trickles quietly by in the dryer months of summer; its banks are being cleared and water-loving plants introduced. Elsewhere, clearance is underway, too, and by opening up long-hidden areas, wild flowers have been given space and light to thrive. A charming pergola with its own seat has been built at one end of the garden to add vertical interest and a touch of formality. The recent loss of some mature trees near the house has been a blessing in disguise – it has created open spaces where there was once too much shade. Jos, a kitchen designer, and Mary-Anne have planted rhododendrons, azaleas, camellias and many flowering shrubs and everything is being designed to blend with the peaceful setting and the backdrop of grand old trees. A collection of David Austin roses has been introduced – his are the only ones which seem to do well here, Mary-Anne says. There's plenty of colour too, with varied colour themings from one border to the next.

The house is named after the hill and the peace within is as deep as the valley. You have utter privacy, a private entrance to your own fresh, elegant suite: a twin-bedded room and a large, square, high sitting room with double doors giving onto the wooded valley. There's a CD player, plus music, chocolates and magazines and you can have tea in the rambling garden that wraps itself around the house. Jos and Mary-Anne really want you to enjoy your stay; you will. Butcher's sausages and free-range eggs for breakfast. Perfect.

Rooms:
1 twin, en suite (bath/shower) with sitting room and adjoining single for child if needed.
Price:
£30 p.p. Single supp. £10.
Meals:
Dinner, 3 courses, £18 p.p., by prior arrangement. B.Y.O wine.
Closed:
Christmas & New Year.

From Launceston, B3254 towards Liskeard. Go through Daw's House and South Petherwin, down steep hill and turn last left before little bridge. House is first on left.

A FASCINATING PROJECT in garden archaeology. Huge efforts have been made to restore the stately 1835 grounds of the Gothic/Elizabethan-style mansion, magnificent in its spectacular setting. The gardens were originally designed and made by Edward Kemp who trained under Joseph Paxton – of Crystal Palace fame – at nearby Chatsworth House. A nice touch of history in reverse is that the gardener who helped Bobby in the early stages of the great scheme has now moved on to Chatsworth. The Hull-Baileys have Edward Kemp's original design and planting plan and their first idea was to replicate it in all its details. An ambition too far, Bobby says now, but their compromise, to interpret the original, is working well. Kemp capitalised on the position by creating the terrace gardens from which you may gaze down to the river below and across to the countryside beyond. The garden is utterly of its time, with elegant balustrades, a parterre tapestry, lawns so emerald-green you hesitate to walk on them. Each of the beds has been restored to its original outline. Bobby comes from a family of keen gardeners and says modestly that she was the only one who didn't show an early interest and isn't a gardener by nature. She's catching up fast. She and Len have chosen good perennial plants for many of the formal beds and used a judicious selection of annuals to adorn others. The result is a brilliant period piece.

Cressbrook Hall

Cressbrook, nr. Buxton, Derbyshire SK17 8SY

Tel: 01298 871289   Fax: 01298 871845
stay@cressbrookhall.co.uk
www.cressbrookhall.co.uk

Bobby & Len Hull-Bailey

A magnificent William IV property built on the precipice of a spectacular limestone gorge. Beyond the formal gardens and 30 acres of parkland there are panoramic views over the River Wye and to the green hillside of Brushfield beyond. Inside, sympathetic renovation is complete – you'll marvel at the ornate, delicate plasterwork on the ceilings. Imposing though it is, this former mill owner's house today buzzes with family life. Four generations of Hull-Baileys live here. Bobby cares for guests and family alike with efficient kindness.

Rooms:
2 doubles and 1 twin, all en suite
(bath and/or shower).
Price:
From £32-£47.50 p.p.
Meals:
Dinner & packed lunch,
by arrangement.
Closed:
Christmas & New Year.

From Ashford-in-the-Water, B6465 to
Monsal Head. Left at Monsal Head
Hotel, follow valley to The Old Mill,
fork left. Left, at lodge building with
white fence and 'Private Drive' sign.

MARGARET AND ROBERT are dedicated, skilful, knowledgeable gardeners and their talents are abundantly clear from the moment you arrive. Margaret is a true plantsman who knows and loves her plants; Robert is the garden architect. He has added delightful touches, including a pergola fashioned from the iron pipes of the old greenhouse heating system and fences made from old holly branches. Exploring the garden is enormous fun – there are so many surprises. The sloping site includes a woodland garden, hot sun terrace, rockeries, pools, a fern area, a jungle garden, mixed borders and an exquisite ornamental kitchen garden. The Fords are keen on evergreen shrubs and have an interest in euphorbias. They have a particularly unusual collection of herbaceous perennials and are always on the lookout for fresh treasures to add to their collection. Statuary peeps out at you in unusual places and all around the garden are strategically placed seats where you can soak up the varied displays. The overall theme is one of informality, with walls, terraces, paths and well-planted troughs hidden from each other. Lovely in spring, gorgeous in the full flower of summer, good autumn colour and winter interest, too, from their huge collection of shrubs.

Horsleygate Hall

Horsleygate Lane, Holmesfield, Derbyshire S18 7WD

Tel: 0114 289 0333
www.sawdays.co.uk

Margaret Ford

Wake up to the sounds of hens, ponies and doves as they cluck, strut and coo in a charming, old stableyard outside. The house was built in 1783 as a farmhouse and substantially extended in 1856; the garden was once home to the hounds of the local hunt. The house is elegant yet relaxed and full of antique country furniture and subtle colours. Breakfast is served in the old schoolroom and is a feast of organic eggs, honey, home-made jams and garden fruit from Margaret's superbly maintained kitchen garden. Glorious setting... and place. Children over five welcome.

Rooms:
1 double, en suite (bath/shower);
1 family and 1 twin sharing
bathroom & wc.
Price:
£22-£24 p.p. Single occ. from £28.
Meals:
Available locally.
Closed:
23 December-4 January.

Leave M1 at junction 29 and take
A617 to Chesterfield, then B6051 to
Millthorpe. Horsleygate Lane is 1
mile on, on right.

Barkham

Sandyway, Exmoor, Devon EX36 3LU

Tel: 01643 831370   Fax: 01643 831370
adie.exmoor@btinternet.com   www.sawdays.co.uk

John & Penny Adie

You eventually come to a deep, 'secret' valley to discover the rambling Georgian farmhouse of artist John and wife Penny. Crisp and white outside, it's homely and informal inside, with an oak-panelled dining room, antiques and paintings everywhere; there are long views down the wooded valley from the rooms across the gardens. John is proud of his musically gifted family – Penny sings and their daughter is a harpist; they stage concerts here each year. The en suite bedroom is large and lovely; the other two rooms are much smaller. Children over 12 welcome.

NOTHING CAN PREPARE YOU for the great surprise of Barkham. Walk through the courtyard archway and suddenly you're confronted by the most wonderful, secret valley view you could imagine; it comes completely out of the blue. This is blissful arcadia improved by some sturdy hard landscaping and the planting of hundreds of trees. Tons of earth were moved by a JCB to create a level lawn between the patio and the sloping grass beyond as a wide platform to sit, relax and admire the natural beauty before you. John has channelled the plentiful hillside water below the lawn into sparkling streams – banked by some of the local shillet stones he has found in the garden – and created a series of small waterfalls. The sound of water is everywhere as you walk down the grassy slope towards the valley below. Above the house is a spick-and-span vegetable garden by an orchard packed with good trees including cherry, plum and apple. Climb up a stone staircase with Alchemilla Mollis drooping over the edges to the charming little cottage garden – pretty, traditional and completely in keeping. Tree peonies, tall spurges, roses and cottage flowers bloom in profusion. John always has some project or another on the go and at the time of writing, he had just completed a dry stone wall planted with aubrieta among the self-seeding pennywort. Nothing is fussy, all is tranquil.

Rooms:
1 twin and 1 double, sharing bathroom;
1 king-size, en suite (bath/shower).
Price:
From £23-£30 p.p.
Single supp. £5.
Self-catering £250-£550.
Meals:
Packed lunch £5 p.p.
Dinner, 3 courses, £18 p.p.
Closed:
Christmas.

A361 to Barnstaple. Right at junction of South/North Molton. Through N. Molton, over bridge, onto moor signed Sandyway. After 3.5 miles, left at x-roads to Simonsbath; after 400yds right down lane, signed.

DYNAMIC GARDENERS, TONY AND LIZ are making a fascinating garden in the six and a half acres around their new home – a Georgian farmhouse on a warm, south-facing site. It's a lovely mix of the classically formal and gently informal, a wide wildflower meadow and two acres of natural parkland wood. They have only been here since mid-1999 and the work they have put into the grounds is stupendous. Within a year they have transformed what was, until recently, no more than a field. By the house is a quarter of an acre, landscaped and charmingly designed formal garden with a spring-fed pool, a pleached lime walk, handsome borders, a pergola for roses and wisteria and yew hedges already taking shape. In direct line with the front door, a bold, straight grassy avenue has been cut, leading you down the gentle hillside, then a side path leads you to the woodland which Tony and Liz are restoring, thinning and re-planting, encouraging wild spring flowers to reappear. There is also a wildlife pond with ducks, dragonflies, fish and dipping swallows. They are keen plant collectors, so there are new plants everywhere, along with trees, spring bulbs, herbaceous beds – they have made more than 4,000 plantings in their first 12 months alone. They love and encourage wildlife and you'll find an abundance of birds, even a tawny owl. A wonderful garden in an unspoilt setting.

Lower Hummacott

Kings Nympton, Umberleigh, Devon EX37 9TU

Tel: 01769 581177   Fax: 01769 581177

Tony & Liz Williams

How did Tony and Liz manage to create a garden and complete the massive renovation and decoration of their delightful home all at once? Fireplaces were opened, decorative ceiling panels added, new bathrooms installed and wooden columns and panelling set into the fabric of the house. All is welcoming, all looks as if it has been here for years. Bright, fresh colours, antique furniture, charming decorative touches with pretty papers. Fresh fruit and flowers in bedrooms and a deeply inviting kingsize bed in one. Dinner is superb: organic and traditionally reared meats, local fish, organic own vegetables, free-range eggs and home-made cakes, biscuits and jams.

Rooms:
1 double and 1 twin/double, both en suite.
Price:
£25 p.p.
Meals:
Dinner £16.50 p.p.
Closed:
Occasionally.

From M5, take A361 to Tiverton. There, take B3137. 3 miles on, B3042 to Eggesford and turn right for A377. 5 miles on, take B3226. 1 mile on, right for Kings Nympton. Go through village; house on left, 0.5 miles on.

DOCTON MILL'S FAMOUS GARDENS in an Area of Outstanding Natural Beauty are a much-loved Devon attraction – eight acres of natural woodlands, lawns and trees. If you haven't already visited these grounds, you may have spotted them on TV in one of many gardening programmes. Lana and John have recently taken them over and they are showing the same devotion to the grounds as did the previous owners. The mill is ancient, and the garden has been developed since the 1930s. The mill stream and a river run through the grounds and the bog garden, created to take full advantage of all this water, is exceptional. It's a garden for all seasons but the spring displays are particularly gorgeous. The grounds have more than 10,000 narcissi flowering from February to May besides a mass of wild flowers, primroses, daffodils and bluebells. Established and new magnolias, camellias and rhododendrons bloom profusely against a backdrop of mature woodland. Banks are shrouded with luscious ferns. There's a little courtyard by the house where cream teas are served among banks of herbaceous plants, and a lower, grassed meadow with a collection of rare apple trees. Beautifully maintained paths lead you to explore and enjoy the carefully-worked theme of bountiful planting among natural beauty and, above all, the restful, restorative magic of running water. A wonderful garden which Lana and John are caring for with skill and energy.

Rooms:
1 double and 1 twin,
both en suite (1 shower, 1 bath).
Price:
£34.50 p.p. Single supp. £10.
Meals:
Dinner £25.50 p.p.
Closed:
Christmas-New Year.

From North Devon, A39 to Hartland/Stoke. Follow brown/white flower signs for house. From North Cornwall via A39, left at the West Country Inn, follow signs for Elmscott. Straight on at YHA, house is signposted.

Have these lovely grounds to yourself in the evening and early morning. Sit on your own private veranda outside the large beamed sitting room with the working mill-wheel turning below. Gaze down from the large, peach-coloured double at foxgloves and ferns thriving by the stream. Beds are old and comfy, brass in the double, traditional iron in the blue-and-white striped twin. Breakfast is served in the sitting room, dinner in the large dining room, in which log fires burn during winter. All is fresh, cosy and unfussy, and Lana and John are friendly hosts who love nothing more than chatting about their lovely garden.

Docton Mill

Lymebridge, Hartland, North Devon EX39 6EA

Tel: 01237 441369   Fax: 01237 441369

john@doctonmill.freeserve.co.uk   www.doctonmill.co.uk

Lana & John Borrett

WADE THROUGH WAIST-HIGH herbaceous plants, follow winding paths – their edges hidden by flopping leaves and flowers – and gaze at the glorious views from the formal wrought iron, gazebo-like pergola; draped in wisteria and laburnum, this was constructed with design help from Rosemary Verey. The grounds were first planted in the 1970s as a one-acre garden around the house, with a wide range of shrubs and trees, including pieris, azaleas, camellia, viburnum and mahonia. In the past decade the garden has been extended to about four acres, and designed to melt into the Devon countryside. The house is 1,000 feet above sea level so John and Maureen have chosen a wide range of traditional hardy plants and trees with a few exotics sprinkled about in the more sheltered places. Two acres have been devoted to native trees surrounding a simple flowering meadow to encourage wildlife. Spring is a lovely time to see the garden – they have planted more than 8,000 bulbs in recent years – and summer sees a riot of growth and colour. Autumn brings beautiful foliage displays and in winter, the sweet scent of mahonia and viburnum hangs in the air before the first double snowdrops appear. There really is a year-long magic. As John says, it's a wild, friendly, relaxed garden with lots of interest but not a whiff of pretentiousness.

Rooms:
3 four-posters, 2 en suite
(1 shower, 1 bath), 1 with private
shower room.
Price:
£32.50-£35 p.p. Single supp. £10.
Meals:
Packed lunch £5 p.p.
Closed:
Christmas & New Year.

Exit A30 at Okehampton & Belstone.
Follow signs for Belstone. In centre of
village turn right after red telephone
box. After 0.75 miles cross cattle grid.
Next house on left.

The 14th-century, Grade II-listed, thatched Devon longhouse within Dartmoor National Park was recently home of author Doris Lessing. Its history goes on and on... enchantingly pervasive in the architecture, interiors, gardens – and atmosphere. Sleep resplendent in four-posters in low-ceilinged, beamy rooms, all with views of the very English country garden whence come copious fresh flowers. Your hosts are adventurously well-travelled and interesting. Just one field away lies the moor with all its wild treasures.

Tor Down House

Belstone, Okehampton, Devon EX20 1QY

Tel: 01837 840731   Fax: 01837 840731
tordownhouse@gofornet.co.uk

John & Maureen Pakenham

HEAVENLY. NO OTHER WORD. James has created a masterpiece in his valley garden, a place of so many delights and such glorious informality and plantsmanship that even on a cold, wet June morning it was hard to tear oneself away. Black swans glide on the large pool fed by the stream which runs through the garden, a pair of amiable turkeys gobble on the lawns and nuthatches bully more timid birds at the bird table. And that's before you have discovered the wonderful contrasts in every corner. The garden is mature and informal and in perfect harmony with the architecture of James' home and with the charm of this hidden, wooded valley. Lovely roses climb up the façade, good shrubs thrive everywhere and herbaceous borders are piled high with colour and leaf. One secret place leads to another, with shaded, private sitting places; reflect and become overwhelmed by the natural beauty which surrounds you. James calls this a cottage and pond garden but it is much, much more. It's an exquisite celebration of nature, from the rare breeds of poultry and decorative pheasants to the fabulous collection of plants he has introduced so skilfully over the past 20 years. An all-weather tennis court is secreted away and you'll even find a table tennis table under a tree. And you can stay in these grounds – there's a gipsy caravan complete with its own double bed!

Map No: 1

Silkhouse

Drewsteignton, Exeter, Devon EX6 6RF

Tel: 01647 231267

James Clifton

A dazzling, eclectic style energises the long, rambling 16th-century longhouse, named by Huguenots who wove silk here. Fine furniture, lovely pictures everywhere, richly decorated bedrooms in mulberry, terracotta and pink. If you're in the 'Boat Room', don't forget to duck below the deeply bowed ceiling. Dine or breakfast in the beamed, low-ceilinged dining room beneath a vast brass chandelier; rest or read by a large granite fireplace with views of the garden. A wonderful place.

Rooms:
1 double with private sitting room,
1 double and 1 twin, all en suite.
Price:
£25-£30 p.p. Single supp. £5.
Meals:
Dinner, 4 courses, £15-£18 p.p.
Light supper by arrangement.
Closed:
Never.

M5 junction 31 onto A30 towards Okehampton. 10 miles on, left signed Cheriton Bishop. 4 miles on, first left after going over the dual carriageway. Through tunnel and immediately right, follow lane to bottom of hill.

Tor Cottage

Chillaton, nr. Tavistock, Devon PL16 0JE

Tel: 01822 860248   Fax: 01822 860126
info@torcottage.co.uk   www.torcottage.co.uk

Maureen Rowlatt

YOUR FINAL APPROACH to the house is along a half-mile, tree-lined track that's so long you'll wonder if you've taken the wrong turning. Your persistence is rewarded with a sudden burst of light and colour as you arrive at this lovely hideaway home. Birds sing, dragonflies hover over ponds and buzzards patrol the skies in that lazy way of theirs. Maureen has created this idyllic corner from what was no more than a field with a stream running through it. She has managed to make use of leylandii in a way in which even its staunchest opponent would approve and shaped it into a perfectly-manicured 20-ft high L-shaped hedge which effectively shields the heated swimming pool and adds welcome privacy. A series of paths and steps lead you to new delights – flowers, shrubs and plants chosen for leaf texture and colour and all beautifully maintained. There are secret corners, too, particularly by the stream and in a dappled wood with its very own, wonderfully slug-free hosta garden. Two of the cleverly converted outbuildings used for bed and breakfast have their own little gardens. Natural woodland and a recently made path up the wooded hillside are bonuses. A year-round fairytale garden – from the first wildflowers of spring to the icy white of winter frosts.

Luxury touches at every turn – as if the rare solitary stream-side setting of this longhouse wasn't enough. Maureen pampers you imaginatively: champagne on occasions, toiletries, bedside bags of truffles, soft towels and robes in huge bedrooms – one with its own conservatory, the other two with private terraces. Outdoors, a swimming pool is colourfully lit at night. Renowned for inspired vegetarian and traditional cooking, Maureen serves breakfast in the (fountained) sunroom. She is gregarious yet unobtrusive. Moors, not fairies, at the bottom of the gardens. But there is magic here....

Rooms:
3 garden rooms, each with private garden or private conservatory, 2 doubles, 1 twin/double, all en suite (bath or shower).
Price:
£57.50 p.p. Single occ. £89. Minimum 2 nights. Special winter breaks November-March.
Meals:
Restaurant nearby.
Closed:
Christmas & New Year.

In Chillaton keep pub and P.O. on your left, up hill towards Tavistock. After 300 yds, right turn (Bridlepath sign). Cottage at end of lane.

Corndonford Farm

Poundsgate, Newton Abbot, Devon TQ13 7PP

Tel: 01364 631595
corndonford@btinternet.com   www.sawdays.co.uk

Ann & Will Williams

Pure ancient magic! Ann is wiry, twinkly and kind. She has restored this listed Devon longhouse with its Bronze Age foundation, keeping the shippon end (where her gentle giant shire horses live) and creating an engagingly chaotic haven for innumerable furry friends and the B&B guests whom she and Will so enjoy. Simple but snug bedrooms, one with a four-poster. Her shire horses will pull you in a wagon to discover the lanes and picnic spots of the Dartmoor she knows so deeply. The house is right by the Two Moors Way footpath. Children over 10 by arrangement.

CLIMB AND CLIMB THE DARTMOOR EDGE with views growing wider and wilder all the time until you reach the stone-walled lane and the sturdy granite buildings of Corndonford Farm. Roses and wisteria clamber up the rugged façade, softening the ancient strength of the house. At jam-making time the air is filled with the sweetness of an enormous pan of bubbling strawberries. Ann's jewel-like little farm garden has an arched walk of richly scented honeysuckle, roses and other climbers which leads to her very productive vegetable and soft fruit garden – the source of the berries. She knows her plants and has created a small, cottagey garden in complete harmony with its surroundings. There's a rockery and a little, gravelled patio just outside the house which has been planted with charming cottage flowers. Above is a lawn edged by deep borders absolutely packed with colour and traditional cottage garden plants, including salmon pink rhododendron, cranesbills and lupins. Do take the very short walk along the lane to Ann's second garden, known locally as the 'traffic calmer'. Here, by the roadside, she has planted loads of rhododendrons and shrubs in a delightful display – and it really does encourage even the most hurried motorists to slow down. The views are breathtaking, the setting wonderfully peaceful, the garden as informal and welcoming as Ann and Will themselves.

Rooms:
1 four-poster and 1 twin, sharing private bathroom.
Price:
£20 p.p. No single supp.
Meals:
Packed lunch, by arrangement.
Closed:
Christmas.

From A38 take 2nd Ashburton turning towards Dartmeet & Princetown. In Poundsgate pass pub on left & take 3rd signposted turning right towards Corndon. Straight over cross-roads, 0.5 miles further & farm is on left.

TWISTING LANES AND A STEEP HILL lead to secluded Dodbrooke Farm in its rural valley setting. Since John and Judy moved here from Kent 17 years ago – they farmed and grew fruit – they have made the most of the glorious natural beauty all around. Dartmoor looms above distant trees and a rapid stream winds its way through this charmingly informal garden – a magnet for birds and other wildlife. A little island, reached by a wooden bridge, is now a secret garden planted with rhododendrons, hydrangeas and camellias which thrive in the acid soil. Wild flowers grow in profusion and are cherished, Muscovy ducks waddle and swim in the sparkling stream. Trees grow well here so John and Judy have created their own arboretum in an adjacent field and dug out a pond. A little orchard produces apples, plums and soft fruit and a very productive organic kitchen garden supplies the house with most of its vegetables. Two little cider orchards provide the fruit for freshly made apple juice and traditional cider. As Judy says, they're not fussy about garden plants but they are utterly devoted to making the very most of the setting. On bright spring days, masses of daffodils bloom; in summer the acid-lovers come into their own. Perfect peace with the soothing sound of running water in a fabulous setting.

Rooms:
2 twins and 2 singles, all with basins and sharing 1 bathroom.
Price:
£20 p.p. Under 2s free,
under 5s half-price in parents' room.
Meals:
Evening meal occasionally available, £10 p.p.
Closed:
Christmas.

Travelling south west, leave A38 at second Ashburton turning; follow signs for Dartmeet. After 2 miles, fork left to Holne. Pass church on right. After 240m, right; after 150 m, left to Michelcombe. Left at foot of hill.

"Very special people and a lovely place to stay in the middle of nowhere," says our inspector. The Hendersons' 17th-century longhouse has a gorgeous cobbled yard, goats and a family atmosphere. They produce their own moorland water, all their fruit and vegetables and even make cheese. The rooms are attractively simple and in country style, with a cosy sitting room for guests and dining room overlooking the garden. The attitude is very 'green' (hedge-laying, stone wall-mending) and the conversation always good.

Map No: 1

Dodbrooke Farm

Michelcombe, Holne, Devon TQ13 7SP

Tel: 01364 631461

John & Judy Henderson

MERILYN AND PHILIP ARE BOTH passionate about their eight-acre garden, always planning new features and displays to add to Wadstray's charms. When they came in the early 1990s, both house and garden needed major renovation but, on the plus side, they inherited plenty of mature planting; this was the work of Viscount Chaplin, a leading member of the Horticultural Society. He planted vigorously and well in the early 1950s, hence the profusion of good shrubs and trees including magnolia, camellias, azaleas and rhododendrons. The garden is open and sunny, with lovely valley views which they have improved by extending the lawn and moving a ha-ha fence to open up the vista even further. By the house, with its colonial veranda, Merilyn has created a gorgeous herbaceous border which blooms in profusion in summer. Spring displays get better all the time thanks to a continuing programme of bulb planting. Woodland areas have been slowly cleared to give more light, older shrubs pruned back to encourage vigorous growth. Lots of good hydrangeas – Merilyn and Philip are gradually adding to their collection because they do so well here. An new acer glade has now been established to give autumn colour. Beyond the lawn is a wildflower meadow leading to a wildlife pond and a walled garden which attracts alpinists from miles around who come to buy plants from the specialist nursery.

Map No: 1

Wadstray House

Wadstray, Blackawton, Devon TQ9 7DE

Tel: 01803 712539   Fax: 01803 712539
wadstraym@aol.com

Philip & Merilyn Smith

Wadstray, a solid, early Georgian Grade II-listed country house, was originally built as a gentleman's residence for a merchant trading in the nearby seafaring town of Dartmouth. Everything here has an air of substance. The bedrooms have balconies, or canopied beds, or sea views. There are open fires in the dining room and a fine library for rainy days. There is the mood of a secret garden with a self-catering orangery with its own creeper-clad ruin... and behind it all a long valley view bridged by a distant strip of sea.

Rooms:
1 double and 2 twins, all en suite.
Price:
From £27.50 p.p. Single supp. £15.
Meals:
Available locally.
Closed:
Christmas Day & Boxing Day.

From A38 take A384 for Totnes. Follow signs for Totnes, take A381 to Halwell, then turn left by Old Inn pub. At T-junction, left onto A3122. House is 0.5 miles past Dartmouth Golf & Country Club, on the right. Do not take Blackawton village turning.

Nonsuch House

Church Hill, Kingswear, Dartmouth, Devon TQ6 0BX

Tel: 01803 752829   Fax: 01803 752357
www.sawdays.co.uk

Christopher Noble

*The view is staggering. From your wicker seat in the conservatory, or
as you look out from the little lawns, you can spy the whole of
Dartmouth below and a fleet of yachts at their moorings. To your left
the mouth of the Dart is guarded on both points by ancient castles.
But Nonsuch does not rest on its natural laurels. Everything about it
is captivating. The guests' sitting room has its own balcony, there are
great fresh breakfasts, large and extremely comfortable beds in big
airy bedrooms and sparkling top-quality bathrooms.* Children over
10 welcome.

THE VERTIGINOUS GROUNDS OF NONSUCH HOUSE
presented Christopher and his green-fingered
mother Patricia with the hugest of challenges, and
there isn't a garden-lover who won't applaud and
love all they have achieved. This is inspired
gardening. The garden is formed like a tall, dizzy-
making staircase with narrow rectangular levels,
culminating in a flourish of palms, an orchard
where apples provide fruit for fresh apple juice
and a huge, shady gunnera. The garden is hot,
hot, hot – from the top terrace with its containers,
little box hedges and colourful borders to the final
terrace three levels below. Even lemon trees look
right. It would have been so easy to rely on the
stunning view and ignore the awkwardly shaped
grounds, but the Nobles would have none of that.
Christopher's hard landscaping is a joy – levelling,
backing up beds with railway sleepers, sowing
lawns, creating flower beds. Hedges of beech have
been planted to give definition and shape,
architectural trees introduced, wooden staircases
built so that guests can explore this extraordinary
creation. Spiky cordylines and flourishing hebes
are a little reminder that the Nobles are Kiwis and
love plants from their homeland; most of the
plants have been raised from seed or cuttings by
Patricia. Stands of agapanthus, a narrow herb bed
for culinary use, pretty herbaceous beds – all
skilfully arranged to make the most of the
garden's dramatic site and view.

Rooms:
3 twins/doubles,
2 en suite (1 bath, 1 shower),
1 with private bathroom.
Price:
£35-£40 p.p. Single supp.
by arrangement.
Meals:
Dinner, 3 courses, £21.50 p.p.
Cheese course, £4.50 p.p.
Closed:
Never!

2 miles before Brixham on
A3022, take A379. After 2 miles
fork left (A3205) downhill,
through woods, left up Higher
Contour Rd, down Ridley Hill.
Nonsuch House at hairpin-bend.

ONE FASCINATING ACRE LEADS to a reeded inlet of Poole Harbour and their own SSSI where, if you're lucky, you'll spot a Dartford Warbler among the gorse. The garden has been created from scratch over the past 30 years and carefully designed to make the most of the views over heathland – haunt of two species of lizard – and water. Liz is a trained horticulturalist and she and David have capitalised on the mild weather here to grow tender plants – copious additions of compost and horse manure have improved the sandy soil. These tender treasures thrive gloriously and are unusually large – you're greeted by a huge phormium in the pretty entrance garden by the drive – mimosa, cordyline and hibiscus do well, too. Acid-lovers are happy, so fine displays of camellias and rhododendrons among hosts of daffodil and tulips once the sweeps of snowdrops have finished. Three borders are colour themed – each represents a wedding anniversary: silver, pearl and ruby. Kitchen gardeners will be knocked out by the seriously good vegetable garden. Play croquet on the large lawn, explore the private woodland where David has created winding paths, relax in the shade of the gazebo or in the warmth of the working conservatory, admire the many unusual plants or simply sit back and enjoy the colour and interest around you... and that shimmering view.

Rooms:
King-size four-poster
(bath and shower); twin (bath);
small double (shower). All en suite.
Price:
£21-£33 p.p. No single supp.
in small double. 10% off for 3 nights,
15% for a week.
Meals:
Dinner £12-£18 p.p., by arrangement.
Closed:
Occasionally.

From Upton x-roads (0.5 miles S.E. of A35/A350 interchange), turn west into Dorchester Rd, second left into Seaview Rd, cross junction over Sandy Lane into Slough Lane, then first left into Beach Rd. House is 150 yds on, on right.

The house takes its name from the place where fishermen brought their craft ashore, in the unspoilt upper reaches of Poole harbour. The three guest bedrooms all face south and make the most of the main garden below and the views beyond. Elizabeth and David's green fingers conjure up a mass of home-grown produce as well as flowers – vegetables, jams, eggs, herbs and fruit; the food is fabulous. Guests can linger in the antique oak dining room; there are log fires and a lovely, huggable grey dog, a Weimaraner called Tess.

Lytchett Hard

Beach Road, Upton, Poole, Dorset BH16 5NA

Tel: 01202 622297 Fax: 01202 632716

David & Elizabeth Collinson

Old House

Fordstreet, Aldham, Colchester, Essex CO6 3PH

Tel: 01206 240456   Fax: 01206 240456   www.sawdays.co.uk

Patricia & Richard Mitchell

THERE'S NOTHING LIKE OPENING your garden to the public to focus on what needs attention. Today the two-acre garden behind this gorgeous house is a delight – its rear façade a rampant display of wisteria and the winter-flowering clematis cirrhosa. The mood changes with every turn: open lawns, a large wildlife pond, gravel areas, herbaceous borders, a corner where wildflowers bloom, a charming 'secluded' garden. The sunny garden faces south west and the planting by the house is hot, hot, hot, with the bright colours of the crocosmia Lucifer particularly eye-catching in later summer. An area has been recently planted with a handsome collection of old-fashioned roses which thrive well in a corner of England where lack of rainfall can be a problem. Richard has given his artistic tendencies full rein on the tall leylandii hedge which encloses the croquet lawn, sculpting shapes into the top. Leylandii has its uses, particularly when you need shelter from the keen east winds which endanger more tender plants in this part of England. The overall mood is of a much-loved, large-scale cottage garden, constantly evolving, informal and with good plants. Can the Colchester road really be just the other side of the house? You wouldn't know.

As fascinating as the area it lives in, the Grade II*-listed 'Old Hall' House has two mainly 14th-century cross wings, and a 'new' 15th-century wing where you breakfast in front of the log fire. A forest fell, surely, to provide the beams. The bedrooms are cosy and welcoming, with undulating floors and 'museum corners' enshrining original features. The road goes close by but there is the enchanting garden and good insulation. The interior is as beguiling as the house itself, with wonderfully strong colours. Think of beams, sofas, handsome furniture, books and a sense of history, and immensely likeable hosts.

Rooms:
1 double/family room, en suite (bath); 1 twin with private bathroom; 1 single with separate shower room & wc.
Price:
Family room £45-£55, with £5 supp. for camp bed. Twin £20-£25 p.p. Single occ. £27.50-£32.50.
Meals:
Available locally.
Closed:
Never.

On A1124, 2.5 miles west of A12 junction. House is on left beyond the Cooper's Arms and opposite Queens Head. Parking in courtyard.

SALLY'S SUNNY TWO-ACRE GARDEN suits this tall, rugged, handsome 16th-century stone farmhouse. Nothing whacky, no new-wave effects, instead a pleasant series of well-tended formal and informal areas setting off both house and its position against a wooded hillside. Originally laid out in the 1930s, the garden's present form was created in the 1950s/60s by a previous owner. The centrepiece is a long Italianate garden which follows a long lawn edged with lush herbaceous borders to a cool, hedge-enclosed canal. Across is a strait-laced rose garden of the old school built around a square pool guarded by four sentinel-like yews cut neatly into shape. A young arboretum is springing up near water features including a deliciously water-lily-choked pool and then ha-has draw the eye across fields to the southern tip of the Cotswolds. The enclosed orchard is an oasis of dappled light that gleams with spring flowers, hot areas around the house are generously planted and Sally's potager-like vegetable garden is a charming blend of the functional with the decorative. She grows colourful, as well as standard, veggies and herbs and a clever touch is added by a pair of diamond-shaped lavender beds. Boyts is not a plantsman's garden – although there are many good plants – instead, it is a warm, welcoming, generous traditional English country house garden which treats its architecture and surroundings with respect.

Rooms:
1 double and 1 twin, both en suite (bath).
Price:
£35 p.p.
Meals:
Available locally.
Closed:
21 December-2 January.

At M5 junc. 16, A38 for Gloucester. After 6 miles, take Tytherington turn. From north, leave M5 at exit 14 and south on A38 towards Bristol. Tytherington turning after 3 miles. Farm is off Baden Hill Road.

Views of the garden everywhere, whether from wide staircase or rooms. The guest sitting room is scented with wood fires and the dining room has a fireplace, oil paintings and large mahogany table. The windows are mullioned and there's a strong sense of country life, from the sound of horses outside to horsey prints indoors. One delightful eccentricity is the perfectly preserved 1950s bathroom with fishy wallpaper. Flagged floors, panelled walls and a spotless interior complete a ravishing picture. Typically caring, Sally insisted I park in the shadow of a horse trailer when I arrived. Lovers of both horses and gardens will be utterly at home.

Map No: 1

Boyts Farm

Tytherington, Wootton-under-Edge, Gloucestershire GL12 8UG

Tel: 01454 412220 Fax: 01454 412220
jre@boyts.fsnet.co.uk
www.sawdays.co.uk

John & Sally Eyre

Millend House

nr. Newland, Coleford, Gloucestershire GL16 8NF

Tel: 01594 832128   Fax: 01594 832128
apriljohnt@aol.com

John & April Tremlett

NATURE'S GARDEN – that's what they call the Forest of Dean – and you have to agree with the sentiment. Here you have a plant-lovers' garden overlooking the valley to Newland. Whichever way you approach the house, you enjoy a glorious drive. April was a flower demonstrator for the NAFAS (National Association of Flower Arranging Societies) for 25 years so, as you'd expect, she's chosen interesting foliage and plants with strong form and texture. The two-acre garden she and John have made over the past 35 years is packed with gems. One acre is woodland with mostly deciduous forest trees, one gloriously smothered with the rampant rose, Treasure Trove. Explore the winding woodland walk which in turn entices you up to the head of the hill and then down past delightful, informal arrangements. A wide variety of shrubs and perennials in a series of profuse descending displays and some intimate touches too, like the tiny Italian garden with its formal stepped area, the little Japanese garden at the start of the woodland walk and small scree bed garden. The kitchen garden is just as attractive. The garden is regularly open for charity.

Lots of curiosities here in the Tremletts' 1750s home and all sorts of amusing ups and downs and in and outs because it's built on a hill; the architectural solutions to this challenge are all part of its charm. The rooms are bright and cheerful and the original semicircular cupboard in one of the doubles is a gem. A friendly, family home with hosts whose love of plants and gardens is infectious.

Rooms:
2 twin/doubles, en suite;
1 double, with private bathroom.
Price:
from £25 p.p.
Single supp. £7.50.
Meals:
Available locally.
Closed:
Occasionally.

From Bristol, A466 towards Monmouth. In Redbrook, right signed Newland. 0.5 miles past Newland, bear left signed Coleford. 300yds on, 2nd house on right. Park in orchard on left, not in front of house.

THE HAUNTINGLY ATMOSPHERIC Edwardian landscaped grounds would make a perfect setting for open-air Shakespeare – rather apposite since it's said that young Shakespeare roamed the hills around Stinchcombe. Hugh's grandparents laid out the grounds, influenced by a love of Italian gardens and admiration for Gertrude Jekyll. When Hugh and Crystal moved here, the garden was distressed and needed attention, particularly the magnificent topiary. The beautifully varied, lofty, sculptural yew and box hedges, domes and busbies dominating the view from the house are restored to perfection, creating a series of garden rooms with a backdrop of woodland. Paths and a romantic Irish yew walk invite you to wander as you move from one compartment to the next. By the house, a pergola is covered with wisteria in spring and rambling roses in summer near displays of lovely old roses underplanted with lavender. Crystal describes these two acres as informally formal or formally informal – she can't quite decide which. But it's that elegant Edwardian design with its Mediterranean mood which makes Drakestone House so special. The best moments to enjoy the grounds are on sunny days when the shadows play strange tricks with the sculptured hedges and trees... expect Puck or Aerial to make a dramatic entrance at any moment!

Rooms:
2 twins and 1 double,
1 with private bath/shower &
2 with shared bathroom.
Price: £31.50 p.p. Single supp. £5.
Meals:
Dinner £17.50 p.p. B.Y.O wine.
Closed:
December-January.

From Stinchcombe take B4060 to Wootton-under-Edge. Go up long hill, house is at top on left – the gateway is marked.

A treat: utterly delightful people with wide-ranging interests (ex-British Council and college lecturing; arts, travel, gardening) in a manor-type house full of beautiful antiques and furniture. The house was born of the Arts and Crafts movement – the architect was Oswald P. Milne and the two thatched cottages in the grounds were designed by Ernest Gimson – and remain fascinating: wood panels painted green and log-fired drawing room for guests, quarry tiles on window-sills, handsome old furniture, comfortable proportions... elegant but human. Refined but easy.

Map No: 1

Drakestone House

Stinchcombe, Dursley, Gloucestershire GL11 6AS

Tel: 01453 542140   Fax: 01453 542140

Hugh & Crystal St John Mildmay

Frampton Court

Frampton-on-Severn, Gloucestershire GL2 7EU

Tel: 01452 740267   Fax: 01452 740698

Henriette Clifford

A superb Grade I-listed house, without pretension to modern luxury, in a fascinating village. The house speaks the elegant language of Vanburgh, is beautifully crafted (do study the stonework outside, the carving and panelling inside) and the Strawberry Hill Gothic orangery (self-catering and pictured above) is stunning. Choose between two large rooms: one with Flemish tapestry, double-tester bed with hand-embroidered curtains and dressing room; the other a twin with views, antiques and panelling. Best of all for garden-lovers, the original Frampton Flora paintings, in pristine condition... gorgeous!

Map No: 1

FRAMPTON COURT HOLDS A SPECIAL PLACE in the hearts of wild plant lovers. It was here that the charming Henriette Clifford's great-great-aunts recorded almost half the wild plants in the parish between 1840 and 1870 in some of the finest amateur plant paintings. Scrapbooks of the pictures were discovered in an attic in 1982 and became the subject of Richard Mabey's best-selling *The Frampton Flora*. Many of these flowers can still be found in the large grounds, a deeply romantic relic of early 18th-century formal gardening. A path below a copper beech leads through wild flowers to the ornamental Dutch canal and an exquisite orangery. Water lilies, lazy carp and wild geese from the nearby Slimbridge Wildlife Trust thrive here. Behind the house are huge views to the edge of the Cotswolds across fields and a lake so large that many mistake it for the nearby River Severn. Low beech hedges, bottle-shaped Irish yews and an arch embraced by roses draw the eye to the landscape beyond. Henriette apologises for today's simplified beds and borders; she can recall an age when labour-intensive gardening was very much part of life in grand country houses. No apology is needed. A visit to this historic place firmly planted in British botanical history is a pilgrimage and a privilege.

Rooms:
1 twin, en suite; 1 tester bed, with single and private bathroom.
Price:
£45 p.p.
Meals:
Good restaurant opposite and 2 pubs on village green.
Closed:
Never.

Leave M5 at junction 13 and follow sign for Frampton (2 miles). Left at r'bout, right opposite Esso garage. Left down village green. Entrance on left between 2 chestnut trees.

Hampton Fields

Meysey Hampton, Cirencester, Gloucestershire GL7 5JL

Tel: 01285 850070   Fax: 01285 850993

Richard & Jill Barry

Map No: 2

RICHARD AND JILL BARRY are making a garden as exciting and as individual as their incredibly ambitious conversion of a derelict barn into a beautiful home. Friends thought they were mad when they left their village house with its gorgeous garden for the empty three acres and abandoned stonework of Hampton Fields... now they've changed their minds. This is dynamic, naturally evolving large-scale country gardening of a very high order. Not a single sheet of graph paper was used; instead the design flowed in a naturally evolving process. Jill loves old roses, herbaceous perennials, interesting shrubs with good leaf features and attractive trees. She and Richard have introduced thousands in a series of fascinating areas which culminate in fan-shaped avenues of the decorative pear Pyrus calleryana 'Chanticleer'. You arrive to a riot of self-seeding hollyhocks and other sun-lovers thrusting through gravel and will find it easy to relax in the well-planted sunken garden with its charming fountain and hexagonal pond. Beyond lie lawns, attractive herbaceous borders and an orchard underplanted with climbing roses. There are roses, too, on trellises, walls and arches, mingling with intoxicatingly scented honeysuckle. The garden's water level rises and falls alarmingly and the natural pond in the main garden can become a sheet of floodwater; Richard and Jill have met this challenge and many more by trial and error and with great imagination.

In a delightfully unspoilt area of the Cotswolds, this attractive, long stone house sits in splendid, peaceful isolation. Lovely high windows in the central part give onto the views and from the soft green-painted conservatory you can admire the garden that the Barrys have so lovingly created. Inside, the décor is fresh – so are the flowers – the furniture and books old, the charming owners happy and proud to have you in their home. Beds are incredibly comfortable with excellent sheets and pillows.

Rooms:
1 double, en suite (bath);
1 twin and 1 double sharing bath and shower.
Price:
£30-34 p.p. Single supp. by arrangement.
Meals:
Excellent pubs nearby.
Closed:
Christmas, New Year & Easter.

From Cirencester A417 towards Lechlade. At Meysey Hampton crossroads left to Sun Hill. After 1 mile, left at cottage. Hampton Fields is 400 yards down drive.

Winstone Glebe

Winstone, Cirencester, Gloucestershire GL7 7JU

Tel: 01285 821451 Fax: 01285 821451
sparsons@cablenet.co.uk

Shaun & Susanna Parsons

Map No: 1

A COTSWOLD GARDEN with aristocratic bones. It was laid out by Dame Sylvia Crowe, author of Garden Design (1958), a mover and shaker of her time and a founder member of The Institute of Landscape Architects, in a rather formal manner with stone walls and a barrier yew hedge. Shaun and Susanna – the gardening fan – moved here in the mid-1970s inheriting only Michaelmas daisies and a red hot poker. Now all is transformed. The bones are softened with luscious herbaceous borders and wilder areas where spring flowers give vivid colour. A recent addition is a little arboretum of unusual trees in a paddock opposite the house. In an impetuous and utterly vindicated moment of inspiration, she recklessly shoved one shaky drystone wall into the field below to create a ha-ha and opened up the view to the Saxon church below. Horses in the field now lean across the ha-ha to nibble spring flowers, but Susanna is good humoured about it. Daughter Harriet, who discovered a love of gardening while working for Rosemary Verey at Barnsley House, now studies at Kew. She pops back bearing unusual treasures to add horticultural interest and help her mother achieve an easy, colourful mood which suits the time-worn architecture of their home. Relish the intimate view to the church and, on clear days, the glorious panorama of the Marlborough Downs.

Delightful Susanna, who has been looking after guests for 10 years will create traditional favourites like kedgeree as an alternative to the conventional English breakfast. You'll eat well in fine surroundings – the striking green dining room's long table is surrounded by an eclectic mix of art and furniture. A blazing open fire will lure you into the drawing room of this Georgian former rectory. There's garlanded wallpaper and a desk in the main double and a delightful wardrobe hand-painted by designer Sarah Baxter in the twin. Across the courtyard is a surprise – a large, cheerful, very modern three-bedded room.

Rooms:
1 double, en suite;
1 twin and 1 double,
each with private bathroom.
Price:
£30-£36 p.p.
Meals:
Packed lunch by arrangement.
Dinner £20 p.p.
Closed:
Occasionally.

Winstone is 6 miles NW of Cirencester, off A417. In village follow signs to church. House is just short of church on left on sharp bend by Public Footpath sign.

The Crooked House

Hampnett, nr. Northleach, Gloucestershire GL54 3NN

Tel: 01451 860250 Fax: 0207 385 9243
coraliecowper@yahoo.co.uk

Coralie & Dr David Cowper

With vivaciousness and good humour, the much-travelled Coralie entertains guests in a wing of the listed Crooked House, a house with many nooks and crannies built over the centuries. Breakfast – fresh orange juice each morning – is in the sunny guest dining/sitting rooms surrounded by striking red walls and well-filled bookcases. The bedrooms are bright and cosy with oriental touches from Coralie and David's travels – a friendly antique snake-bearded Sri Lankan mask guards the twin. The view from the double is thrilling. Undulating Cotswold countryside is glimpsed through tall oaks.

COULD THE CROSSROADS of the A40 London-Cheltenham road and the busy Fosseway really be just three quarters of a mile away from this blissfully peaceful hamlet mentioned in the Domesday Book? It is hard to imagine as you explore this well-planted and rapidly developing medium-sized garden. Coralie, who grew up here, has been diligently improving and re-designing the grounds around her historic home – it has been in the family for more than 70 years and parts are 14th-century. A small patio surrounded by profusely planted little beds greets you and you then follow a stone path around the house to a sunny, open lawn, a charming summer house, two ancient yews and a rising sequence of 'rooms' clearly divided by hedges – one a magnificent beech. Enjoy the many treasures to be found in the flower garden, or investigate the peaceful, deliciously informal wild bird garden (Coralie's mother once bred rare macaws that would fly here). In one corner is an ancient Priest's Hole with the tunnel that once linked the house with the nearby church. A paddock is now planted with young, unusual trees which will form a small arboretum and the large vegetable garden is being decorated with a box-edged parterre. Coralie's love for her garden is evident everywhere.

Rooms:
2 twins, sharing bathroom;
1 double, en suite (shower).
Price:
£33 p.p. Special price for Badminton and Cheltenham Week.
Meals:
Dinner £20-£25 p.p., by arrangement.
Closed:
Occasionally.

From A40 Oxford-Cheltenham road, cross roundabout at junction with A429. Hampnett is next left off main road.

When James abandoned his hectic life in the City and moved with Karin to the Cotswolds, he longed to become a garden designer. Today he's a respected historian and successful garden designer, and it shows. They have created a delightfully informal – with a formal touch or two – gently sloping L-shaped one-acre garden wrapped around their 16th-century manor home. The garden is a series of compartments defined by old Cotswold stone walls and hedges of yew, hornbeam, box and cotoneaster, while overhanging trees give welcoming shade on hot summer days. Many good plants have been introduced in an overall design planned for all-year interest, with sparkling displays of rare snowdrops and narcissus and a wide variety of hellebores and species peonies. Summer sees masses of old roses given to them by the late Primrose Warburg and in late summer and early autumn the double borders with their perennials come into their own. Rose arches over a new path are packed with colour and scent, Rosa Cedric Morris scrambles through a walnut tree, the climber, Mrs Honey Dison, covers the children's Wendy House and clematis flowers among apple tree branches. A lovingly designed garden where the Boltons' four children romp, grown-ups can relax and garden-lovers enjoy a fine collection of plants in a beautiful setting.

Rooms: 1 double, en suite (bath/shower); 1 twin/double, en suite (bath).
Price: £30 p.p. Single supp. £15.
Meals: Available locally.
Closed: Christmas.

From Cirencester, A429 towards Stow. Turn right at Bourton Lodge Hotel, signed Clapton. Follow signs. In village, down hill and left at green-doored 3-storey house. Manor is left of the church.

Look over the garden wall as you breakfast on home-made jams and enjoy long views over the valley. The 16th- and 17th-century manor house has a flagstoned hall, huge fireplaces, sit-in inglenooks and Cotswold stone mullioned windows. One of the bedrooms has a secret door that leads to a stunning, surprising fuchsia-pink bathroom. The other, though smaller, has wonderful views of the garden. An easy-going and lovely house with owners to match.

Clapton Manor

Clapton-on-the-Hill, nr. Bourton-on-the-Water
Gloucestershire GL54 2LG

Tel: 01451 810202 Fax: 01451 821804

Karin & James Bolton

Barton House

Barton-on-the-Heath, Moreton-in-Marsh
Gloucestershire GL56 OPJ

Tel: 01608 674303 Fax: 01608 674365

Hamish & Gillian Cathie

Inigo Jones worked his magic on an H-shaped Tudor manor house to create a beautiful house of his period. (The cellars remain untouched, as old as 1200.) Hamish and Gillian welcome small groups of garden lovers who stay for two or three nights and visit some of the great gardens nearby. The glorious guest bedrooms, like their Japanese Garden, show their exquisite taste and passion for the East... two are in Indian style with furniture, miniatures and materials from the sub-continent and the third is Japanese. All have wonderful garden views... perfection!

A SPECTACULAR HOUSE and a breathtaking garden, of dreams brought to perfect reality. Wonderful plants, originality and features which reflect a fascination for the Orient. Gillian and Hamish visited every Japanese garden they could before planning their own and planting it with a host of rarities. The resulting Japanese Garden – their daughter designed the exquisite pagoda – is superb. Move open-mouthed from one gem to another; plantsmen will be green with envy at the huge collection of plants, many rare. The garden was established in 1625 with some of Tradescant's first chestnut trees, replanted in 1850 with Californian Redwoods. The huge Japanese Larch on the back lawn is said to have been planted by the Emperor of Japan and is believed to be the oldest in the country. A useful area of greensand explains the vast collection of rhododendrons and camellias and there are also collections of catalpa, Moutan-tree-paeonies and Stuartia. A rose garden, a little Himalayan garden built around a statue of the kindly elephant god Ganesh, a woodland garden with a Catalpa Walk, formal lawns, an arboretum, a vineyard… there is much to see and admire. Lots of ornamental ironwork, too, created by the estate blacksmith (who diversified after developing an allergy for horses!).

Rooms:
3 twins, each with private bathroom.
Price:
£60 p.p. Single supp. £25.
Meals:
Dinner £30 p.p.
Closed:
Occasionally.

From Stratford-upon-Avon on A3400, 16 miles south turn right at Long Compton, follow sign to Barton by church. Barton House clearly marked opposite village green.

Mill Dene Garden

Blockley, Moreton-in-Marsh, Gloucestershire GL56 9HU

Tel: 01386 700457   Fax: 01386 700526
wendy@gardenvisit-cotswolds.co.uk   www.gardenvisit-cotswolds.co.uk

Wendy Dare

WENDY KNEW ALMOST NOTHING about gardening when she and Barry bought their tumbled-down mill as a weekend retreat from London life 35 years ago. Today Mill Dene's two acres are a magical celebration of plantsmanship and design with the constant, soothing murmur of water from the mill stream. The mill's original garden was a third of its present size and Wendy began her horticultural efforts with a patio by the house. She caught the bug, was inspired by Rosemary Verey's Barnsley House and took gardening classes. She has devotedly extended and improved the garden ever since. All is informal but very carefully planned to make the most of the setting. There is now a sequence of enchanting displays in the sharply sloping, terraced grounds, including a fantastical shell-decorated grotto by the stream. Admire the closely planted beds and borders, her dye plant collection, a little camomile lawn, a bog garden, a smart potager and a cricket lawn for play. Corridors of plants lead you up from the sparkling mill pond to the more open areas above with their Cotswold views. Fragrances everywhere – Wendy is devoted to scented plants and even in darkest winter some delicious scent will come wafting your way. Fragrance, enough interesting plants to satisfy the most demanding plantsman, clever design and a superb setting.

Breakfast on smoked salmon and scrambled eggs, home-made marmalade and local honey in the sunny, plant-filled conservatory and you may see a heron fishing for trout in the mill pond or the electric flash of a kingfisher. The beamed bedrooms have brightly painted or papered walls – William Morris in one. Barry ran Unwin seeds and each bedroom is named after a plant and has its own little original painting for an Unwin packet. Dressing gowns on doors, sparkling bath/shower rooms and, in the large green living room with its huge inglenook fireplace and warm wooden floors, Wendy's home-bred white Birman cats.

Rooms:
2 twins/doubles, en suite
(1 bath, 1 shower);
1 double,
private bathroom.
Price:
£27.50-£32.50 p.p.
Meals:
Available locally.
Closed:
Occasionally.

A44 at Bourton-on-the-Hill follow signs to Mill Dene Garden and Blockley. 1.3 miles down hill turn left, again at brown sign. Mill is 50 yards on right.

Upper Court

Kemerton, nr. Tewkesbury, Gloucestershire GL20 7HY

Tel: 01386 725351   Fax: 01386 725472
uppercourt@compuserve.com   www.uppercourt.co.uk

Bill & Diana Herford

*Life here is elegant, comfortable and peaceful, both indoors and out.
The delightful owners have filled the house with gorgeous things. The
hall has a wonderfully eclectic collection of their talented son's pottery,
old hats, a pair of ancient riding boots. The airy bedrooms with lovely
wallpapers have four-poster beds and immaculate bathrooms. The
house stands behind the parish church and there is an excellent pub
two minutes walk up the lane. In the manor and cottages there are
attractive self-catering options of various sizes. A good place for house
parties.*

Map No: 2

DREAM ON IN THESE MAGICAL 15 ACRES of water, lawns, profuse beds and borders, wonderful trees and secluded enclosed areas. Listen to birdsong, watch ducks, geese and swans glide on the two-acre lake or the mill stream beside the house – the mill is mentioned in the Domesday book. These lovely grounds with their listed 14th-century dovecote and fine outbuildings were re-shaped by the outstanding gardener Marylena Cottrell some 40 years ago to complement the Georgian manor house. She created the lake, developed the walled kitchen garden and planted fine trees. Bill and Diana have continued this legacy with devotion. The immaculate sweep of lawn in front of the house is now a croquet lawn overlooked by mature trees. The walled garden is divided by a tall yew hedge – one side has colourful herbaceous borders and cutting beds for the house, pergolas covered with climbers and a long, perfectly trained vine underplanted with iris. Walk through the yew archway to the other side to discover a swimming-pool garden with a backdrop of well-planted containers and architectural plants. Lawns by the mill stream lead to a large paddock where children play football or cricket and, nearby, Bill has been busy tree-planting beyond the bridge over the stream. The overall effect here is of informal elegance with a combination of intimacy and open areas.

Rooms:
4 four-posters, all en suite (1 shower, 1 bath/shower, 2 bath); 1 twin and 1 twin/double, both en suite (bath). Cottages for 2-8.
Price:
From £42.50 p.p. Single occ. from £65 (weekdays only).
Meals:
Dinner, from £30 p.p., by arrangement.
Closed:
Christmas.

From Cheltenham A435 north, then B4079. About 1 mile after A438 cross-roads, sign to Kemerton on right. Leave road at War Memorial. House is behind parish church.

RAYE IS A PASSIONATE and very skilful gardener and Simon her enthusiastic and self-deprecating assistant. Between them they have recently added a series of fascinating flourishes to the rambling two-acre garden around this Meon valley home. Handsome mature trees provide a backdrop to their creation and, on the lovely wide lawns, where once there was a run-down grass tennis court, there is now an immaculate croquet lawn. Grass paths have been cut through woodland at the far end of the garden, one area sheltering a shaded, pristine hosta bed dominated by a sculpture of a sailfish swimming contentedly among the leaves. The woodland is particularly lovely when spring flowers bloom. Nearby, a bench embraces the trunk of an old yew tree, inviting you to sit and gaze on sunny days. There is a hedge-enclosed, gravel-edged water garden where lilies sparkle in summer under the gentle music of the fountain and four formal beds surround the pond. This leads to the crescendo – a truly stunning formal rose garden. A grassy avenue takes you between lines of wooden rockets enclosing the skilfully trained repeat-flowering shrub rose Moonlight in clouds of the purest white, underplanted with catmint. Pergolas, arches and a series of newly planted yew and beech hedges add form and shape in different areas, and a little box knot garden sets off a deep, dramatically planted border by the house. Lots of places to sit surrounded by flowers as you enjoy an evening drink.

Rooms:
1 double/twin, en suite;
1 double/twin, private bathroom.
Price:
£22.50 p.p. Single occ. £35.
Meals:
From £15 p.p. and available locally.
Closed:
Christmas & New Year.

0.5 miles from centre of West Meon village (on road to East Meon). Home Paddocks on left just beyond bus shelter and telephone box.

The charming Wards have brought the same uncluttered elegance to their home as they have achieved outdoors. The original 16th-century cottage was 'gentrified' by Thomas Lord of Lord's cricket ground fame, with the additions of a veranda and conservatory. Meals are eaten in the salmon-pink dining room with its Delft-tiled fireplace and the large, sunny drawing room has glorious garden views. Bedrooms are pristine but cosy, with dove-grey walls in the larger room overlooking the garden. The many delightful bird paintings are a memento of the couple's days in East Africa.

Home Paddocks

West Meon, Hampshire GU32 1NA

Tel: 01730 829241   Fax: 01730 829577
homepaddocks@compuserve.com

Raye Ward

Land of Nod

Headley, Bordon, Hampshire GU35 8SJ

Tel: 01428 713609   Fax: 01428 717698

Jeremy & Philipa Whitaker

Map No: 2

AN "OH WOW" GARDEN, from the moment you join the long, wide avenue. It strides between lofty stands of pine and banks of rhododendron which introduce you to the seven-acre south facing garden set among 100 acres of private woodland. And it just gets better and better. By the time you reach the white wisteria-clad house you'll by dying to explore these formal and informal grounds. A long history of devotion and a century of family ownership make this is a very special place. Admire the stately trees – the Wellingtonias are believed to be the tallest in the country for their age – and more than a quarter of a mile of superbly tended hedges. The wide, open lawns are perfection. The Japanese garden, created by Jeremy's grandfather in 1901 after a visit to Japan and with a fine collection of mature camellias and acers, is thrilling. Jeremy's enthusiasm is utterly infectious. He's a tree-lover above all, following a family tradition which has transformed a tiny corner of Hampshire into an arboreal paradise of rarities. Even if the botanically uninformed are bewildered by his constant peppering of Latin names, a walk with Jeremy through these part wooded, part open grounds is an experience to cherish. A very special sorbus, a Cedar of Lebanon raised from a seed collected in Les Cedres in the Lebanon, it's all wonderful. And time doesn't stand still. A new camellia grove is thriving, an unusual knot garden is coming to maturity – all speaks of English country-house gardening at its best.

One jewel within another: a fine 1939 house built by Jeremy's father on the site of an old farmhouse and enclosed within ravishing grounds. Breakfast in the chinoiserie dining room with its needlework picture from Kyoto. The tennis court is hidden in the gardens, you can fish, glide and ride locally. Many personal touches in the bedrooms, like the oriental-style bedheads made by the creative Jeremy himself. And, of course, gorgeous garden views from every room. Jeremy is an architectural and garden photographer and they are both natural hosts. The perfect English country house.

Rooms:
2 twins, en suite; 1 twin, private bathroom.
Price:
£30 p.p. Single supp. £10.
Meals:
Available locally.
Closed:
Christmas & New Year.

South on A3 to Hindhead. Straight across traffic lights, after 400yds turn right onto B3002. Continue for 3 miles. Entrance to drive signed on the right.

A PARTICULARLY SPECIAL TREAT FOR GARDEN LOVERS is to visit a garden in the making, particularly one as ambitious as the grounds Angela is developing with the help of talented young designer Josie Anderson from Cheltenham. What was, until not so very long ago, a run-down farmyard area is being transformed into a large, elegant, feature-packed, open sunny garden. It perfectly complements the grand listed Georgian farmhouse which Angela and Hugh have restored, brilliantly, over the past two years. A neglected pond in front of the house has been cleared and planted with water-loving beauties and a second has been created nearby so that as you approach up the drive you see the house in reflection. So much to enjoy once you arrive: an arched walk, a designer kitchen garden, a herb garden, a pretty box parterre, a formal rose garden with the finest roses, a croquet lawn to add green and space. Angela loves flowers and her beds and borders are starting to brim with the most beautiful plants. There's a summer house in which you can unwind and a large conservatory where you can linger and gaze at the splendours outside. On a sunny day, enjoy a swim in the striking L-shaped heated swimming pool tiled in the deepest blue. The setting, in Hallend's 411 acres of farmland, is a delight. Views everywhere – of woodland, open countryside and parkland – in one of the loveliest corners of Herefordshire.

Map No: 1

Hallend

Kynaston, Ledbury, Herefordshire HR8 2PD

Tel: 01531 670225   Fax: 01531 670747
khjefferson@hallend91.freeserve.co.uk

Angela & Hugh Jefferson

*All the grandeur you could ask for from the moment
you enter. The airy hall has a handsome staircase
leading to wide landings and the bedrooms upstairs.
They are large and elegant, with rich curtains, very
comfortable beds and immaculate new bath/shower
rooms. The dining and drawing rooms echo the mood
of classic English elegance. A very friendly welcome
from a couple who have devoted an enormous amount
of care and energy to the restoration of both house
and garden. There are, too, the farm's own lamb,
pork and free range eggs to enjoy.* Children over 12
welcome.

Rooms:
1 double, shower room;
1 twin, bath/shower room.
Price:
£37.50 p.p. Single supp. £10.
Meals:
Dinner, by arrangement,
and available locally.
Closed:
Christmas & New Year.

From Ledbury, A449 west. Right for
Leominster on A4172. 1 mile on, left
for Aylton. 1.25 miles to junction.
Left, follow signs for Nat'l Fuchsia
Collection. Pass it to junction with
Hallend Farm. Keep left, drive first
right.

Winforton Court

Winforton, Herefordshire HR3 6EA

Tel: 01544 328498 Fax: 01544 328498
winfortoncourt@talk21.com
www.sawdays.co.uk

Jackie Kingdon

The staircase, mentioned in Pevsner's, is 17th-century. Most of the house was built in 1500 and is breathtaking in its ancient dignity, its undulating floors, two-foot thick walls and great oak beams. Take a book from the small library and settle into a window seat overlooking the gardens. There is a guest sitting room too, festooned with works of art by local artists. Candles feature all over the house. The two four-postered bedrooms verge on the luxurious; so does the other one. Gorgeous.

A DELIGHTFUL LITTLE WALLED GARDEN greets you at this beautiful half-timbered, early 16th-century house. The path is edged by profuse purple and green sage studded with perennial geraniums, walls carry climbing roses and borders bloom. When Jackie arrived, all the grounds were down to grass with some mature trees and with fine views across the Wye Valley to the Black Mountains. She took heaps of cuttings and potted up plants from her previous home, created borders, planted vigorously and transformed every corner of her big new garden. The sunny courtyard behind the house has a fruit-covered fig tree and mature magnolia, with spiky cordylines in containers, cherubs on walls and a cherub fountain brought from Portugal. Beyond lies her open, terraced garden dominated by a huge weeping willow, with an ancient standing stone on a ley line shaded by a tall horse chestnut, emerald-green lawns, flower-packed beds and, below, a stream being developed into a small water garden. She has even planted the edge of the parking area with colourful sun-lovers thrusting through the gravel. Jackie aimed to make an interesting, informal, open, sunny garden to complement Winforton Court's dreamy architecture, and that's just what she has achieved. Guests love it here – regulars come bearing plants or cuttings for her to add to her plant collection, and are sometimes generously given cuttings of their favourites and a good luck wish that a little bit of Winforton Court will grow in their garden and give them pleasure for years to come.

Rooms:
1 double, 1 four-poster
and 1 suite with king-size
four-poster,
all en suite (bath).
Price:
£25-£35 p.p. Single supp. £15.
Meals:
Available locally.
Closed:
Christmas.

From Hereford, A438 into
village. House on left with a
large green sign and iron gates.

JILL AND MALCOLM BEGAN THIS GARDEN in 1990 and within five years it was featured on BBC TV. Little wonder. The planting is outstanding and the design a clever blend of formal, informal and wild. All this and romantic views to the Black Mountains. Wander through wild meadow where campion sparkles among tall meadowsweet and waving grass, dream in the shady orchard where tea is served under a canopy of trees smothered in rambling roses or watch dragonflies hover over the wild pond. Many schoolchildren have nejoyed visits discovering the perfect natural environment. The more formal features should be admired, too – a large brick-columned pergola weighed down by roses, the rose arch, the lawns edged by beautifully planted, irregular borders. Jill adores clematis and has a collection of more than 150 varieties and has constructed a walk through them all. Maturing hornbeam, yew and beech hedges create a series of areas as you move from one part of the garden to the next – the delight of discovery carries you through. Every hedge, ponds, border, maturing specimen tree and inch of the lawn has been nurtured by the Ainslies and the sheer variety is breathtaking. There are more than 4,000 trees – again planted by the Ainslies – in these magnificent seven acres. The effect of all that hard work is clear.

Rooms:
2 doubles, both with private bathrooms; 2 twins, both en suite (1 shower, 1 bath); 2 doubles, sharing bathroom – in converted stables. Self-catering cottage available.
Price:
From £25 p.p. (minimum 2 nights). Single supp. £5.
Meals:
Dinner, 3 courses, £17 p.p.
Closed:
November-Mid-March.

From Hereford A480 to Norton Canon take lane to Norton Wood & Hurstley. Follow through disused railway arch, sharp bend, past cottages on right. Single track driveway is on left.

All is bright, fresh and simple in the guest rooms in the house and converted barns and stables (the latter divided into B & B and self-catering). The house and outbuildings date back to the 16th and 17th centuries and the ground-floor Garden Room in the house has its own sitting room and garden. The dining room has beamed walls, scroll-carved panels from an old oak cupboard and large old bread oven, now converted into a drinks cabinet. The light-filled conservatory is the perfect vantage point from which to drink in the views of garden and countryside.

Map No: 1

Darkley House

Norton Canon, Herefordshire, HR4 7BT

Tel: 01544 318121   Fax: 01544 318121

Jill & Malcolm Ainslie

A Georgian jewel in a delightful, lofty – 600 feet above sea level – setting. When they arrived, John and Stephanie carefully studied the garden around the house, absorbed its possibilities, assessed where it needed rejuvenation and set to work with huge gusto. The result is a well-considered four-acre country garden. Their master plan was to create gardens within a garden, always with labour-saving ideas in mind. The gardens at the front of the house are a formal introduction to the stunning views and terraced front lawns sweep down to meet the sight of the Wye Valley and the Black Mountains. Beyond is a wildflower meadow divided into two terraces, one of which is guarded by a magnificent, ancient sweet chestnut tree. The old walled garden is approached through a specially commissioned Millennium iron gate which leads to a perfumed avenue of old roses and a sequence of formal parterres. There's a Moghul-influenced area edged by a rectangular rill that contrasts with the silent pool. The rill and other water features use modern pump technology to create yesterday's classic effects. A well-stocked fish pond leads to a long bog garden generously planted with willow and water-loving plants including a gigantic gunnera and the shady shrubbery restored and thinned to give rhododendrons and azaleas room to sparkle. The final flourish behind the house and its 14th-century barn – decorated as a splendid party hall – is a motte-and-bailey topped with an ancient water tower and dovecote.

Bollingham House

Eardisley, Herefordshire HR5 3LE

Tel: 01544 327326   Fax: 01544 327880
bollhouse@bigfoot.com   www.sawdays.co.uk

Stephanie & John Grant

From the sofa in your sybaritically comfortable bedroom you can gaze out on the Malvern Hills and the Black Mountains. In spite of the grandeur of this Georgian house it feels like a real home with large rooms graciously furnished. Fascinating features and furniture everywhere including a timbered frame wall from the original 14th-century house, wide elm floorboards upstairs and a dining room table reputed to be an Irish 'coffin table' which John found in Dublin. Your hosts are delightful and Stephanie's Aga cooking is wonderful.

Rooms:
1 double and 1 twin,
both with private bathrooms.
Price:
From £25 p.p. Single supp. £5.
Meals:
Packed lunch £3.50 p.p.
Dinner £16 p.p.
Closed:
Christmas.

From A438 Hereford/Brecon road towards Kington on A4111 through Eardisley village. Bollingham House is 2 miles up hill on left, behind a long line of conifers.

A DICHOTOMY: 30 MAJESTIC ACRES of lawns, soaring yew hedges, a 19th-century arboretum, a great avenue of Wellingtonia, cedar and other giants and ornamental lakes all set around a mid-1950s home. Anne reveals that the family's Victorian mansion was here until her father, defeated by spiralling costs, had the original Court demolished and re-built his family home in the recycled stone. The grounds were originally designed by William Nesfield in 1858 but have needed total restoration. Mike left ICI so that he and Anne could return to Broxwood to help bring back the grounds to their former glory. They assembled a squadron of the latest motorised equipment to make their grand dreams a reality. Overgrown stands of laurel were ripped out, lawns restored, paths re-opened, huge rhododendrons disciplined and lakes cleared. The recent final touch was decorating the formal rose garden, sheltered by dizzily tall yew hedges, with two drystone slate urns by master craftsman Joe Smith. Anne's Roman Catholic ancestry explains the follies and the names of the avenues – St John's with its St Michael's Walk – and the little Our Lady's Chapel, St Joseph's Hut and Abbot's Pool. Only the occasional scream of white and common peacocks breaks the peace of one of the most unexpected parkland gardens of all.

Broxwood Court

Broxwood, Leominster, Herefordshire HR6 9TJ

Tel: 01544 340245 Fax: 01544 340573

Mike & Anne Allen

Your expectations, as you arrive through the original arched clock tower into the courtyard, are high. Although the house is a modern surprise, it is filled with antiques and fittings from the earlier mansion, including original library bookcases and polished parquet floors. You can settle into the blue drawing room, its open fireplace guarded by two huge porcelain dogs, and breakfast and dine in the red, striped dining room. The bedrooms are charming, with colourful curtains, good furniture and, in the larger of the twins, a huge and ornately-edged padded bedhead and views across to the Black Mountains. Anne, a cordon bleu cook, uses local produce and fruit and vegetables from the organic garden. They are amusing, relaxed hosts.

Rooms:
1 double and 2 twins,
en suite (bath/power shower).
Price:
£33-£38 pp. Single occ. £50.
Meals:
Dinner, £20 p.p.
Closed:
Usually in February.

From Leominster follow signs to
Brecon. After 8 miles, just past
Weobley turn off, right to
Broxwood/Pembridge. After 2 miles
straight over cross roads towards
Lyonshall. After 500 yards, left over
cattle grid.

Lower Bache House

Kimbolton, nr. Leominster, Herefordshire HR6 0ER

Tel: 01568 750304   Fax: 01568 750304
leslie.wiles@care4free.net

Rose & Leslie Wiles

Map No: 1

A LARGE PAINTED SIGN of a Black-veined White butterfly on the main road beckons you down high-hedged, narrow lanes to the utter peace and seclusion of Rose and Leslie's home and garden. Leslie is a butterfly-lover – he has his own butterfly house and hopes to help re-introduce the lost Black-veined White; their favourite plants, like Red Valerian, are encouraged in this charming, informal cottage garden. The whole place is undergoing major changes: a new formal pond, a herringbone-bricked herb garden and a flight of steps to the private nature reserve and wooded valley below are just the start. A large pond is planned and a garden room with reclaimed oak-framed windows is to be added to the valley side. The little orchard is being extended with new trees and the series of beds are a mass of cottage garden favourites, such as red, pink and white foxgloves. Peppery-scented lupins grow in cheerful stands in unfussy, densely planted beds and borders. Tall busbys of box stand guard in the pretty lawned side garden, overlooked by screens of taller conifers to bring intimacy. Part the side branches of a large, sweet-smelling philadelphus and you open a natural door to the sunny front garden which welcomes arriving visitors. The Wiles encourage birds and wildlife: an owl box has been built on a gable, swallows swoop in and out of the eaves, doves, swifts and chattering starlings nest in the roof every year. A delightful, natural garden and a place of real tranquillity.

An utterly fascinating place. The 17th-century farmhouse, cider house, dairy, granary and 14-acre nature reserve are perched at the top of the small valley; the views are tremendous. In the huge dining room is the old cider mill, and dinner may feature the Wiles' home-smoked fish or meat and home-made bread. Much of what they serve is organic – all the wines are. One room is across the courtyard, the other three in the granary annexe; they are all timber-framed, compact and well thought out and have their own sitting rooms. Children over eight welcome.

Rooms:
4 suites (2 doubles, 2 twins), each with sitting room and bath/shower room.
Price:
£29.50 p.p. Single occ. £29.
Meals:
Dinner £15.50-£21.50 p.p.
Closed:
Never.

From Leominster, take A49 north but turning right onto A4122, signed Leysters. Lower Bache is then signed.

GUESTS HAVE BEEN KNOWN TO JOIN IN THE WEEDING, so infectious is the enthusiasm of Amanda and Guy for their garden with its handsome lawns and mature trees. The couple couldn't garden in Guy's service days but he took early retirement from the RAF and, once work on the house was complete, they relished turning next to the garden. Their best legacy was the collection of fine mixed deciduous and evergreen trees – Victorian maps describe the grounds as a Plantation and Victorian diarist Francis Kilvert records playing croquet here in 1871. Over the years the Plantation had become overgrown; areas were choked by brambles or hidden under laurels, so a cut-and-burn programme began. Today Amanda and Guy are brimming with plans big and small and putting them into practice. Borders are being extended, raised beds re-planted, new shrubs introduced and saplings added to the orchard with its collection of traditional varieties of English apples and other fruit. Guy is determined to be self-sufficient in fruit and vegetables and is developing his two kitchen gardens, one by the all-weather tennis court. Above all, they are striving successfully to make these grounds blend naturally and elegantly with the surrounding pastureland.

Map No: 1

The Old Vicarage

Leysters, Leominster, Herefordshire HR6 0HS

Tel: 01568 750574 Fax: 01568 750208
guy.griffiths@virgin.net
www.sawdays.co.uk

Guy & Amanda Griffiths

This is one of the three remaining 'tranquil' areas of England (says the CPRE), 18 acres of which are the grounds and garden of this 17th-century farmhouse. Victorian additions brought generous, high-ceilinged spaces. Antiques, old paintings and large, high beds with crisp white linen add to the comfort. Guy not only grows the fruit and veg but also bakes the bread. Amanda loves cooking and sharing meals with guests around the huge dining table. Wonderful, and in a very lovely, surprisingly undiscovered, corner of England. Children over 12 welcome.

Rooms:
1 twin, en suite (bath);
1 double, en suite (bath/shower).
Price:
£34 p.p. Single supp. £10.
Meals:
Packed lunch by arrangement.
Dinner, 3 courses, £19 p.p.
Closed:
Occasionally.

House 1 mile south of A4112 between Tenbury Wells and Leominster. On entering Leysters from Tenbury Wells, left at x-roads in village. Ignore sign to church. House on left, through wooden gate (after postbox in wall).

IS THE SENSUALLY UNDULATING LAWN just an example of modernistic landscaping? Not a bit of it. 'Worples' is a corruption of 'wurples', Kentish for ridge-and-furrow and the wave-like lawn patterns around which Sue has built her garden are very far from modern, and hugely intriguing. Sue is a garden designer and it shows. She makes interesting use of large garden 'furniture' – a traditional Shepherd's hut here, a little 100-year-old summer house from Alastair's grandmother's garden there. And that is just the start. In 1997 she began a serious re-design of these three-acre grounds with their beautiful views across the valley. No corner is untouched by her flair and her plans are starting to bear fruit. The new orchard is underplanted with bulbs, the wildflower meadow is beginning to blossom, the trees and fine shrubs she has introduced are fleshing out beds and borders. There's a lily-pad shaped pond for frogs, newts and damselflies and an avenue planted with winter-flowering cherries and azaleas. The original sunken garden just below the house is being lovingly re-designed around an 'orb' sculpture of sun and planets with its surrounding beds planted with hot colours for planets – red for Mars among them, of course. The vegetable garden has been transformed into an ornamental potager. Every feature enhances the view and entrances. Sue's favourite season is autumn, when the garden is in harmony with the landscape beyond, but every season is a delight in this young garden.

Rooms:
1 twin, with private bathroom;
1 twin and 1 double, sharing
bathroom (shower/bath).
Price:
£25 p.p. Single occ. £40.
Meals:
Available locally.
Closed:
Christmas & New Year.

A25 eastbound, take first left (after sign for Westerham and red stripes on road) into Farley Lane. House at the top on the left.

Sue is likely to greet guests in her wellies and gardening clothes at her home above a steep valley. You are only 22 miles from central London, yet immersed in much of historical, geological and architectural interest. The house was built in the 1920s by a local architect in a style typical of the area and period. Bedrooms are bright, towels soft and colours restful; the bedrooms that share the bathroom have a lovely view. Relax in the garden room full of scented plants, and Sue will spoil you with home-made treats.

Worples Field

Farley Common, Westerham, Kent TN16 1UB

Tel: 01959 562869

marr@worplesfield.com   www.worplesfield.com

Sue & Alastair Marr

THE GARDEN WAS DESIGNED in the 1920s when this medieval and Tudor farmhouse, massively extended in Edwardian times, had a staff of seven gardeners! No more. Mervyn and Jane today devote their considerable energies to what they call "gardening on a shoestring", when not caring for their guests in their lovely home. With 20 rolling acres – some woodland, fields and pleasure gardens and a hillside wild garden to care for and restore – their efforts are Herculean and will be admired by every garden lover. The grounds reflect the house – rambling, time-worn, romantic. Avenues are cut through deep grasses to emphasise glorious views across the surrounding countryside and deep borders are piled high with herbaceous plants. Jane's greatest love is the steep wildlife garden where she is cutting her way through a jungle of over-mature rhododendrons and sweetly-scented azaleas. Stone paths are being rediscovered after many years of neglect, water features cleared and restored. This wild area was - and is still – a place where children are at their happiest and which is shared with deer, foxes and rabbits. Acid-lovers thrive here; magnolias and camellias do especially well. Now that her family has grown up, Jane is devoting more and more of her time to her vast garden, and her enthusiasm shows in every corner. Nothing fussy, everything informal, a laid-back approach to developing the grounds with limited manpower. Don't expect showiness, do enjoy the atmosphere of a garden that has been blessed with a new lease of life.

Map No: 2

Hoath House

Chiddingstone Hoath, nr. Edenbridge,
Kent TN8 7DB

Tel: 01342 850362
jstreatfeild@hoath-house.freeserve.co.uk

Mr & Mrs Mervyn Streatfeild

*In May, the scent from the azaleas and
rhododendrons is intoxicating. But even the glories of
the garden cannot diminish the impact of this
part-Edwardian, part-Tudor house. The Streatfeilds
have been in Chiddingstone for centuries – the castle
was their seat – but carry their history lightly. They
are well-mannered, intelligent, easy folk. Some
furniture is well-worn and faded but everything feels
authentic. Bedrooms are huge, with views over the
gardens, grazing sheep and hills. You can settle into
the fireside chairs in the library. Everything for
children, too. It's worth every penny.* Minimum 2
nights' stay at weekends.

Rooms:
Main house: 1 twin and 1 double
with shared bathroom.
Annexe: 1 double, en suite (bath).
Price:
Twin/double £27.50 p.p.; single occ.
£25-£35. Reduction for
2 nights or more.
Meals:
Light suppers and dinners £9-£16 p.p.
Closed:
Christmas & New Year.

From A21, N. Tonbridge exit. Follow
signs to Penshurst Place, then to vineyard.
Pass vineyard, then right at T-junc.
towards Edenbridge. Through village,
bear left (following signs to Edenbridge).
House is 0.5 miles on left.

AN OAST HOUSE IN THE GARDEN, a Grade II Wealden part-brick, part tile-hung former farmhouse. This is an intimate, charming corner of High Weald countryside which David and Margaret have worked hard to embellish both indoors and out since they moved here in 1983. The garden is almost two acres with a fine layout, thanks to a previous owner's friendship with gardens' writer Christopher Lloyd. The planting, however, was a little past its best and needed attention. Everything changed in one terrifying crescendo with the Great Gale four years after David and Margaret arrived. Mature trees were torn aside, the garden blasted, but they turned adversity into advantage, using newly-opened areas to introduce new shrubs now reaching handsome maturity. The long, open lawn leads to a little stream and tiny valley where a pond was being planned at the time of writing. Interesting initiatives with plants everywhere – there's a growing collection of old-fashioned roses and a drive heavily planted with spring flowering bulbs. The herbaceous borders near the house set off the architecture nicely, giving floral detail and contrast with the tree planting at the far end of the garden. David recently took early retirement from the City and his growing enthusiasm and skill in gardening is reflected everywhere. A professional kitchen gardener would be hard put to equal the efforts that go into the vegetable garden *and* it has stunning cutting flower beds.

Rooms:
1 double, with private bathroom;
1 twin, en suite.
Price:
£25-£27.59 p.p.
Meals:
Available locally.
Closed:
October-March.

On A21, 5 miles south of Tunbridge Wells, turn left onto A262 signposted Goudhurst. 2 miles on, right into Bluecoat Lane, signposted Kilndown. At minor crossroads, right into Ranters Lane. House is first on right.

A mini-library of very good garden books awaits you outside the bedrooms so you can mug up before or after Sissinghurst and other local delights in this garden hotspot of Kent. Breakfast in style beneath a brass candelabra in a dining room decorated with striking, very effective American blue-flowered paper. Bedrooms are pretty and pristine, one in Colefax and Fowler floral, the second in gentle shades of pale – and there are cut flowers from the garden in season, too. Enthusiastic hosts, in a friendly family home.

Map No: 2

Mount House

Ranters Lane, Goudhurst, Kent TN17 1HN

Tel: 01580 211230
davidmargaretsargent@compuserve.com

David & Margaret Sargent

A SMALL, LAWNED, BORDERED and railed front garden by the stuccoed High Street façade, a long walled town garden behind the red-brick rear frontage – two utterly different worlds. Jane has gardened assiduously since she moved from country to town 20 years ago. Until she came to Deacons, she had a four-acre farm garden with woodland. It was, she says, quite a culture shock, but she has adjusted well and learned the very different discipline of creating an urban sanctuary by working ever-deeper borders around the lawn. She has skilfully broken up the stern rigidity of a typical rectangular back garden space by introducing curving edges, tall growing shrubs to give height and a bed dividing the lawn into two areas. Strong focal features include a large urn on a noble pedestal. She adores old-fashioned roses and always asks friends and family to add to her collection on important birthdays and celebrations. Another passion is for clematis – Jane has dozens and reckons that there is hardly a day in the year in which at least one clematis is not in bloom, from the subtle charm of winter's evergreen cirrhosa to the showier blooms of summer. Walls and fences have been carefully planted to soften the surroundings and give extra privacy. Good plants jostle for attention, colour is everywhere. Delightful.

Rooms:
1 twin and 1 single, sharing bathroom.
Price:
£27.50-£30 p.p. No single supp.
Meals:
Available locally. Dinner/supper,
by arrangement.
Closed:
December-February.

From Maidstone, A229 towards Cranbrook. Take left fork for town centre. Next left into High Street. House is approx. 300m on left.

Jane once farmed fruit and cattle; the superb naïve pictures of bucolic cows remind her of her days in an old beamed farmhouse. Today she is a charmingly informal hostess, her home is elegant, pristine Regency, with good furniture, cosy bedrooms – one with very bold floral wallpaper – and comfy beds. Staffordshire dogs peer down from the tops of cupboards and shelves. Eat breakfast looking over the garden from the dining room, or watch life go by on the historic High Street from your own little sitting room.

Map No: 2

Deacons

High Street, Cranbrook, Kent TN17 3DT

Tel: 01580 712261

Jane Wilson

Breakspears Road

London SE4 1XR

Tel: 0181 469 3162   Fax: 0181 469 3162
bunzl@btinternet.com   www.sawdays.co.uk

Biddy Bunzl

Map No: 2

IF BIDDY HAS BROUGHT A WILDLY COLOURFUL new twist to B & B, her partner, New Zealander James Fraser, brings something different to modest-sized town garden design with his funky planting. He dreamed of creating a corner of South Island, New Zealand in South London. He has his own plant business, specialising in NZ plants, and is an acclaimed town-garden designer for adventurous clients looking for the unusual. His own garden certainly flies the flag for his original ideas. You're greeted by yuccas in window boxes, a snaking path to the front door and strikingly different plants in the small front garden. Step out of the wooden-floored kitchen/breakfast room at the back to follow his wooden paths and push your way, explorer-like, through head-high grasses and a forest of antipodean plants and tall fans of thrusting planks reaching heavenwards. Everything you pass is exotic – spiky phormiums and cordylines sit with many rarities which are a perfect expression of James' passion for the plants of his native country. All the wooden structures – the fans, the pond fashioned from chunky railway sleepers, the decks and sculptures – are made of wood collected from stretches of London's empty docklands. Local wildlife is drawn to the garden's sense of sanctuary, while gardeners delight in the shock of the new.

This is fun! A house-cum-gallery in a conservation area where each room exhibits original, modern art. Bedrooms have all the useful things that you don't want to lug around town with you – radio, hairdryer and alarm clock. Bold colours, wooden floors, huge curtain-less windows and indoor trees give an exotic feel. Breakfasts are cooked on the Aga and eaten in the vast and stylish kitchen with deck views over the subtropical garden (breezy days are a bonus as tall grasses ripple and sway). Biddy, kind and easy-going, has brought a breath of fresh air to the world of B&B.

Rooms:
1 twin, en suite (shower).
Price:
From £30 p.p.
Meals:
Dinner by arrangement.
Closed:
Never.

From Brockley station, cross Brockley Rd & walk up Cranfield Rd. Cross Wickham Way at church & continue along Cranfield Rd. Breakspear's Rd meets it almost opposite. Free on-street parking.

24 Fox Hill

Crystal Palace, London SE19 2XE

Tel: 020 8768 0059 Fax: 020 8768 0063
timhaigh@compuserve.com

Sue Haigh

Sue has moved since she appeared in the 4th edition of our *Special Places to Stay: British Bed & Breakfast*. Her new home is in the sweet seclusion of Fox Hill – the artist Pissarro lived close by in his London days and painted the street and the tree opposite. The small gravelled front garden has bobbles of box and a recently planted paperback maple – an eye-catching frontage for the pretty Victorian house – but there's much, much more to come. The long rectangular back garden has been completely re-designed and now bursts with colour and interest in every direction. Sue, who once worked at the Chelsea Physic Garden and is a true plant-lover, has cleared and re-planted paved areas by the house and built a raised pond for her beloved fish. The delicate water plants are guarded by tall, spiky agaves which thrust skywards from their containers. Climbers snake up walls, trellises and an arch, while water bubbles soothingly from a water feature. Sue has nurtured a few of the plants that were there when she arrived, a thriving ceanothus and an Albertine rose among them, but otherwise started with a clean slate. To add a final flourish and to mark her pleasure at having her first-ever garden shed to play with, she has planted a Liquid Amber sweet gum outside its door. This is a young garden packed with promise.

Rooms:
1 double/twin, en suite;
1 single and 1 twin,
sharing shower room.
Price:
From £40 p.p.
Meals:
Lunch £15 p.p.
Dinner, 2 courses, £15 p.p.,
3 courses, £20 p.p.
Closed:
Never.

This part of London is full of sky, trees and wildlife; Pissarro captured on canvas the view up the hill in 1870 and the original painting can be seen in the National Gallery. There's good stuff everywhere – things hang off walls and peep over the tops of dressers; bedrooms are stunning, with antiques, textiles, paintings and big, firm, new beds. Sue, a graduate from Chelsea Art College, employs humour and intelligence to put guests at ease and has created a very special garden, too. Tim often helps with breakfasts.

Main line trains from
Victoria or London Bridge –
20 mins to Crystal Palace,
then 7 mins walk. Sue will
give you directions or
collect you. Good buses to
West End and Westminster.

A GAZEBO MADE FROM local stone gazes out across 1.5 acres of open, sunny, informal garden with wonderful views across rolling fields and woods and the neighbouring Althorp estate. Caroline and John are keenly conscious of the garden's setting and have designed it to make the most of those views and to complement the elegance of their unusual 1950s Georgian-style home. The garden was created from a field when the house was built and then sympathetically redesigned in the mid-1980s. The roadside wall is a mass of aubretia with flowering trees and the wide gravelled drive leads to an angled façade which sparkles with wisteria, clematis and climbing roses. Borders overflow with maturing shrubs and a kaleidoscope of leaf colours – the spring displays are gorgeous and if you're staying in early spring don't miss the copse beyond the tennis court, cleverly masked by tall copper beech hedges. The little glade is a carpet of snowdrops in season. Soothingly wide lawns, the terrace and, for added interest, intimate garden 'rooms' with surprises hidden by mature hedges, all work in harmony. Breakfast on sunny days on the patio, surrounded by sweet-scented flowers and admire one of the garden's showstoppers: the mature Laburnum Adamii, which puts on a spectacular display of pink and yellow flowers.

Ridgway House

Great Brington, Northampton,
Northamptonshire NN7 4JA

Tel: 01604 770283   Fax: 01604 770022
caroline@studiog.demon.co.uk

John & Caroline Gale

Caroline's parents orchestrated the building of this elegant home – their architect designed the private apartments at Chatsworth. You're greeted by a pair of jolly Jack Russells in a very unusual six-sided hall with a grand slate and portland stone floor. Breakfast in the dining room, relax in the family atmosphere of the large drawing room. The bedrooms have pale carpets, good furniture, pristine bathrooms and a view to Althorp House through the trees; one has pale colours with wicker furniture, the other bold yellows and greens. You'll sleep soundly.

Rooms:
2 twins, both en suite (bath).
Price:
£35 p.p. Single supp. £10.
Meals:
By arrangement, or available locally.
Closed:
20 December-6 January.

From M1, junc. 16, A45 signed
Daventry. 1 mile on, right signed
Bringtons. In Little Brington, left to
Great Brington, signed East Haddon.
200 yds into Great Brington, house is
behind stone wall as road bends left.

Gowers Close

Sibford Gower, nr. Banbury, Oxfordshire OX15 5RW

Tel: 01295 780348

Judith Hitching

SO HOW DOES A POPULAR English garden writer like Judith Hitching actually garden herself? With great originality and a witty eclecticism that has created a cleverly sophisticated sheltered cottage garden. Only a few years ago, this was an unappetising, bramble-choked half-acre graveyard of dead conifers and heathers. Among Judith's greatest inheritances were the ancient wisteria which clings to the back of her thatched home and some tumble-down pigsties from which she rescued old stone to make paths. When the wisteria is in flower, summer breakfast and dinner on the hot, scented south-facing terrace is unforgettable. There's a touch of formality in the diamond-patterned, box-edged parterre with its wooden obelisks for sweet peas and clematis, but things loosen up with a large herb garden and two lawns, divided by a young yew hedge, sloping gently towards views of the Cotswold hills. The first lawn is edged by four generous, hot-coloured borders; the second is a sanctuary partly shaded by silver birches. A long rose pergola, straddled by four types of clematis and roses, including Iceberg and Himalayan Musk, leads down one side of the garden. Judith enjoys the challenge of topiary and works hard on her intricate box spirals. Scent is very important to her – so prepare to be carried away by the powerful fragrance of lilies and pineapple and mandarin orange-scented salvias. Her favourite flowers? Old roses and pinks, auriculas, those scented salvias and her beloved herbs. From a scruffy bramble patch, Judith has created something memorable for all the senses.

Music, the scent of fresh coffee, dried flowers hung from beams, restful, pastel bedrooms and a deep sense of history – Gowers Close was built in about 1580 and adjoins what was once the Court House. Three tiny rooms, now Judith's larder, broom cupboard and a loo, are thought to have been the village lock-up. Nothing is level here – the many beams and flagstones are all angled by age. This is very much a home and Judith is an amusing, easy hostess who is delighted to chat about plants and garden plans.

Rooms:
1 double with private bathroom; 1 twin, en suite (bath).
Price:
£32 p.p.
Meals:
Dinner £20 p.p.
Closed:
Christmas.

Sibford Gower is 0.5 miles south of B4035 between Banbury and Chipping Campden. House on Main Street on same side as church and primary school.

Upper Court Barn

Millend, Chadlington, Oxfordshire OX7 3NY

Tel: 01608 676375   Fax: 01608 676499
roper-caldbeck@ukgateway.net
www.sawdays.co.uk

Rory & Juliet Roper-Caldbeck

Juliet has coloured and decorated her large, sunny, beamed 17th-century former tithe barn with dramatic bold paint-effect walls. Exotic furniture and furnishings come from their many travels to Thailand, Singapore and India – she loves India and campaigns to save tigers. The main bedrooms are prettily set off by designer wallpapers including Nina Campbell and Colefax and Fowler. Outside, in the courtyard, is the Garden Room which has its own outdoor sitting area and even a sauna. Breakfast in the lofty dining room or outdoors in the courtyard where the garden will tempt you to explore.

Map No: 2

HARD TO BELIEVE that only five years ago, this garden was little more than a farmyard. The space came with the recently-converted Upper Court Barn that was bought from a developer. Rory and Juliet's first move was to plan a tapestry of formal and informal features and they called in a professional gardener friend for advice. Today the garden has come into its own and has all the charms of youth. Rory is the designer, Juliet the chief plantswoman. The formal courtyard garden outside the house is woven around a raised circular pond, the lawn leading to four lavender-edged borders, colour-themed in blues, maroons, whites and pinks. Beyond is a formal vegetable garden with four rectangular beds and an avenue of the yellow-fruited crab apple Malus Evereste. The eye is drawn to a statue by neighbour Briony Lawson, wife of distinguished gardens photographer Andrew Lawson, and underplanted by the darkest grasses. The woodland garden, wildlife pond and wild plant area are starting to come together and further on a long pergola sparkles with roses, clematis and honeysuckle. It all works – it's so well-planned and so meticulously planted, with the nods to modernism in the decorative grasses softened by free, wild areas. A mass of bulbs in spring time, a feast of colour in summer and autumn… a contemporary country house garden.

Rooms:
1 twin and 1 double,
sharing bathroom;
Garden room: twin,
en suite (shower).
Price:
£30-£35 p.p.
Meals:
Available locally.
Closed:
December-February.

From Chipping Norton take A361 south. 1 mile from last 30 mph sign, left to Chadlington. In Chadlington take first right marked Churchill. 70 yards past pub car park sharp right up drive.

MANY ARE THE PLANTS WHICH ENCOURAGE AND FEED BIRDS and other wildlife – the exception are deer which regularly chew a Kiftsgate rose trying to climb an old apple tree. This charmingly informal garden was created from scratch after the Stevensons arrived in the mid-70s. Helen planted interesting shrubs and trees right at the start but further plans had to be shelved for years as children romped and rode bikes in their garden playground. Now the children have grown up, Helen has found more time to focus on gardening and developing this third of an acre surrounded by fields. In spring, the grounds sparkle with generously planted snowdrops, crocus, pulmonaria, sweeps of aconite and drifts of daffodils. Her beloved bluebells are allowed to do their own thing. Those first plantings of trees and shrubs – presided over by an eye-catching golden Acer Platanoides Drummondii – have now come into their own and create areas of dappled light and a fresh, natural feel. Her chemical-free, curved borders and raised beds behind low stone walls are packed with colour – she's a great bargain hunter and eagerly swoops on the plant stalls at her local gardening club. When we visited she was gleefully ripping out a leylandii hedge to replace it with a handsome stone wall... yet another pleasing touch for her colourful, informal English country garden.

Rooms:
1 double and 1 twin,
shared shower room.
Price:
From £23 p.p. Single occ. from £30.
Meals:
Available locally.
Closed:
Christmas.

Take A44 north from Oxford's ring road. At r'bout, 1 mile before Woodstock, left onto A4095 into Bladon. Take last left in the village. House is on second bend in road, only one with iron railings.

Hand-painted Portuguese pottery sits on the dresser in the bright dining room and over breakfast you'll be watched by an amusing collection of wooden birds including an inquisitive lapwing and avocet. The main double guestroom had a make-over for a Laura Ashley catalogue and is as pretty as you'd expect. Guests share a large shower room, so Manor Farmhouse is ideal for families or friends travelling together; the spiral staircase to the twin is steep, but the room feels very private. The family's pet sheepdog Chloe is spoiled by guests – she even receives an annual Valentine's card from one American fan.

Manor Farmhouse

Manor Road, Bladon, nr. Woodstock, Oxfordshire OX20 1RU

Tel: 01993 812168 Fax: 01993 812168
www.sawdays.co.uk

Helen Stevenson

The Lodge

Ludlow, Shropshire SY8 4DU

Tel: 01584 872103   Fax: 01584 876126
www.sawdays.co.uk

Humphrey & Hermione Salwey

THESE ELEGANT COUNTRY-HOUSE GROUNDS are dominated by theatrical cedars, an ancient avenue of sweet chestnuts and grand views, all reached along a sweeping drive. Hermione's courtyard is rarely without huddles of recently bought container plants – she scours nurseries for new additions. The stables and clock tower archway, clad in rosa Banksia and clematis Armandii, lead to the newly created two-acre garden. Wide irregular borders, with shrubs forming a backdrop for tulips, alstroemeria and many different hemerocallis provide spring and summer interest. By August the autumn bed, with crocosmia, grasses, kniphofia, aconites and Michaelmas daisies, is a riot of colour. Some formal flourishes, like the newly planted yew avenue, add a traditional touch in keeping with the grounds. And then comes the best surprise. Pull on your wellies if it's damp and take the steep walk down from the house through fields and trees to admire the Lodge's greatest treasure – a wonderful 18th-century folly garden. A cascade of water drops down to a formal, stone-lined, fast-flowing stream and there's even a crumbling Georgian bath house with a crystal-clear plunge pool. It will fascinate all those who enjoy English romantic garden heritage.

The stupendous site and generous size of this early Georgian house reflect the status of the ancestor who built it in 1740 – the whole house is a gallery of family portraits down the centuries. The present-day Salweys are farmers and Hermione's scrumptious food is based on home-reared beef and lamb and garden vegetables. The large, softly-furnished bedrooms have antique chairs and modern bedding and one has a Louis XV bed.

Rooms:
1 twin and 1 double, en suite (bath); 1 double with private bathroom.
Price:
£40 p.p. Single supp. £5.
Meals:
Dinner £20 p.p.
Closed:
31 October-1 April.

From Ludlow, over River Teme by traffic lights, 2nd right to Presteigne & Richard's Castle on B4361. After about 100 yards, drive is first right.

LOVELY, GLORIOUSLY GREEN-FINGERED JANET has lost count of the number of different plants crammed into her intricate tapestry of gardens. From an unprepossessing acre of barren land and builders' rubble she has created this enchanting oasis over 24 years. She devotedly labels the scores of more unusual plants to remind herself of their proper name and to inform guests and garden-lovers who come to her charity open days. The setting of this horticultural haven – 1,400 feet above sea level by the Longmynd hills and within 6,000 acres of National Trust land – is wild and spectacular. She is, she says, one of the few to cherish the despised leylandii for the welcome shelter it provides from the winds which whip across the hills. The garden today is a riot of features including scree and rock gardens, sunny lawns, herbaceous borders, an alpine house, shade gardening, secret paths and many nooks and crannies. She's an avid plantswoman, faxing specialist garden centres around the world to collect seeds that she nurtures in her tidy, busy propagating shed. No surprise that most of the plants in her garden are grown from seed and her biggest struggle is to find a space to plant newcomers... but she always seems to find somewhere suitable for them to thrive and do their thing. Plant collectors should make sure they leave room in the boot for new treasures – Janet sells plants to raise money for good causes.

Jinlye

Castle Hill, All Stretton,
Church Stretton, Shropshire SY6 6JP

Tel: 01694 723243 Fax: 01694 723243
info@jinlye.co.uk
www.jinlye.co.uk

Mrs Janet Tory

*Best of all must be the beds – 17th-century French
wedding, Gothic brass, 1940s Italian boudoir – but
the whole converted crofter's cottage has lovely fabrics,
beams and antiques. Run by Janet and her daughter
Kate, Jinlye sits, old, luxurious and sheltered in its
sweep of ancient hills, alive with rare birds and wild
ponies. The skies are infinite; humanity was here
12,000 years ago and you can walk deep in ancient
wilderness before returning to superb home cooking
and a loo with a view.* Children over 12 welcome.

Rooms:
3 doubles, 2 twins/doubles and 2 twins,
all en suite; 1 double with private bath.
Self-catering also available.
Price:
£27-£40 p.p. Single occ. £42-£57.
Meals:
Packed lunch and light supper,
by arrangement. Excellent pubs
and restaurants nearby.
Closed:
Never.

From Shrewsbury, A49 to Church
Stretton, past the Little Chef and right
towards All Stretton. Turn right
immediately past the phone box and
up the hill to Jinlye.

Lawley House

Smethcott, Church Stretton, Shropshire SY6 6NX

Tel: 01694 751236 Fax: 01694 751396
lawleyhouse@easicom.com   www.sawdays.co.uk

Jackie & Jim Scarratt

Map No: 1

MORE THAN 50 TYPES OF ROSE bloom in wild profusion – including a Paul's Himalayan Musk that vigorously scrambles through an acacia. Deep herbaceous borders glow with colour and the secret pond garden with its trickling fountain sparkles with water lilies. Hard to believe that this was a weed-choked three acres of sloping ground when Jim and Jackie came 27 years ago. Since then they have gardened devotedly and imaginatively, creating a richly planted design of lawns, beds, trees and shrubs to draw the eye across the valley to the hill scenery beyond. They began with a massive clearance programme which, to their delight, showed that there had once been a garden here; they unearthed stone steps and, best of all, that long-lost secret pond which they restored. Today the mood is sunny, delightfully informal and traditional – they love colour and scent and have carefully planted to provide all-year interest with a sequence of different sections divided by immaculately tended lawns. Acid lovers, including rhododendrons and camellias, thrive and so do their traditional garden flowers: lupins, sweet peas and delphiniums. No wonder guests can hardly wait to explore this lovely country house garden with its many charms and stupendous vistas – you can even spot the Wrekin on a clear day.

You'll probably be greeted by Bertie, the gentle black Labrador, when you arrive at this large, comfortable Victorian house. You'll receive a warm welcome from Jackie and Jim, too, before being shown to one of the charming bedrooms with uninterrupted views of the Stretton Hills. You can lie in bed in the morning, with the sun streaming in, and gaze over beautiful countryside or enjoy it all from the conservatory downstairs. Then eat a good breakfast before exploring the garden or venturing further afield, on horseback perhaps. Stabling provided and horses can be hired locally. Children over 12 welcome.

Rooms:
1 double with private bath; 1 twin/double, en suite (bath).
Price:
£22-£28 p.p.
Single supp. £10.
Meals:
Available locally.
Packed lunch from £2.50 p.p.
Sandwich supper £5 p.p.
Closed:
Christmas-New Year.

From Shrewsbury, south on A49. In Dorrington, right to Smethcott. After 3 miles, left at x-roads (signed Smethcott). House 0.5 miles on.

PURE POETRY, FROM THE RUGGED, RED-BRICK 17th-century dovecote rising above yew topiary to the charming, beautifully restored, oriental-looking summer house. This is a manorial garden in which grandness and lavish planting have been skilfully combined with natural woodland. The Hall's frontage is a mass of sweet-scented wisteria in season. Gaze across a rising front garden which acts as a ha-ha to give an uninterrupted view of the large, wildfowl-haunted lake edged by pollarded willows. Step around the corner past the dovecote to discover the privacy of what was once a formal rose garden; sheltered by manicured hedges and walls, it has been transformed into a lawned compartment with deep herbaceous borders and old-fashioned shrubs and climbing roses. Walk across the wide, generous lawns behind the house past the summer house into gorgeous woodland. Mature trees blend harmoniously with the many young trees which Christopher and Gill have planted over the years. You are led inexorably through woodland to a delightful, restored ornamental canal. Its banks are a mass of water-loving plants set among shades of green from the tree canopy above. This is a garden for most seasons. In spring you'll see masses of daffodils, crocus and other early flowers and in summer, beds and borders alive with the colour and leaf of thriving herbaceous plants and very good shrubs. Autumn is a riot of golds and reds as the trees and shrubs do their stuff in a final display before winter sets in. Ravishing.

Rooms:
2 doubles, each with private bath & shower. Cottage sleeps 4.
Price:
£30 p.p. Single supp. by arrangement. Cottage from £250 per week. Short breaks available.
Meals:
Packed lunch by arrangement.
Closed:
Christmas & New Year.

From Shrewsbury bypass (A5), B4386 for Westbury/Montgomery. In Westbury, right at cross-roads opposite The Lion pub. First left, 50 yds on, left for Vennington. After 0.5 miles, drive on left and house is at end, on right.

Elegant, never intimidating – mellow brick, cast-iron baths, fading carpets and honey-coloured panelling – and there's a sense of timelessness. Even the breakfasts reflect another age: kedgeree and soft fruit from the garden are seasonal additions. The Georgian bedroom has long views over the carp-filled lake, the other a Chesterfield in its bay window, but do stir yourself to wander through these stunning gardens and the woods beyond. There's a large self-catering cottage, too. Children over 12 welcome.

Map No: 1

Whitton Hall

Westbury, Shrewsbury, Shropshire SY5 9RD

Tel: 01743 884270   Fax: 01743 884158
whittonhall@farmersweekly.net

Christopher & Gill Halliday

The Citadel

Weston-under-Redcastle, nr. Shrewsbury, Shropshire SY4 5JY

Tel: 01630 685204 Fax: 01630 685204
griffiths@citadel2000.freeserve.co.uk
www.citadel2000.freeserve.co.uk

Sylvia Griffiths

Everything is on the grand scale, as you'd expect from your first glimpse of The Citadel in the distance... lofty ceilings with beautiful plasterwork picked out in white against deep colours, an elegant living room with French windows to the garden, a large billiards room with a full-size snooker table and a bright, very large dining room. A great staircase leads up past a ticking longcase clock to the bedrooms, one a riot of rose wallpaper, the others in pale pastels. Baths sparkle with gold clawed feet, pale American quilts cover beds. Dreamy.

Map No: 1

THESE BEAUTIFULLY TENDED, skilfully designed three acres perfectly complement the Gothic Revival architecture of The Citadel and the dreamy rural beauty which surrounds it. The house was built for the dowager Lady Jane Hill who lived at nearby Hawkstone Hall and the garden is full of surprises, so take your time. As the enthusiastic Sylvia says – she and Beverley are devoted gardeners – it's a garden to explore. You'll find new delights at every turn... sweeping lawns with views to Wales and the Shropshire countryside, great banks of lusciously healthy rhododendrons and camellias on a sandstone outcrop, a secret Victorian woodland folly, a charming rustic thatched summer house gazing across fields, woodland walks, an immaculate potager kitchen garden where flowers bloom among the vegetables and a walled, manicured croquet lawn. The delights start by the house with its patio edged by burbling water features and a newly made pergola. You are led past rhododendrons and high hedges to the croquet lawn and kitchen garden and then vanish into woodland with its hidden folly and an acer glade which glows with colour in autumn. Mature trees everywhere: oaks, scots pine and, most spectacular of all, the great copper beech which lords it over the bastion-like façade of this architecturally stunning 1820 folly.

Rooms:
1 double/twin en suite; 1 double, 1 twin, both with private bathroom.
Price:
£38-£40 p.p.
Meals:
Dinner £20 p.p.
Closed:
November-March.

From A49, 12 miles north of Shrewsbury, follow signs to Weston/Hawkstone Park. House is on the right 0.25 miles after taking Hodnet road out of village.

IN THE MID-1980S THIS CHARMING, INFORMAL country house garden, carefully worked to blend in with its lovely rural setting, was a jungle surrounding a derelict house. If there had been a garden before, there were no clues, just masses of rampant vegetation. Four years before Christopher and Tanda bought Greenbanks, the two acres were cleared and sternly disciplined. When they arrived in 1989 they inherited a clear canvas, an open acre with mature trees, a magnolia and just a couple of narrow borders. Both are wildlife-lovers and they have developed the grounds with plants especially attractive to birds, insects and butterflies. "We aimed to create a haven for both wildlife and guests," Tanda says, and they have succeeded brilliantly. The large pond, guarded by an old oak tree, has been cleared and planted with water-lovers (including water lilies), many trees introduced, borders dug and decorated with good shrubs. One of the garden's most charming features is its young woodland planted 10 years ago with mixed native broad-leaved trees, including a grove of silver birch hiding the hard tennis court. The open, sunny, south-facing main lawn has lovely views across the open countryside, and the small walled patio area is a sun trap in fine weather. Judicious planting of many evergreen berried shrubs, winter-flower honeysuckle, bulbs, virburnums, roses and very good herbaceous plants ensure all-round interest. Informal, welcoming, full of interest, a delightful garden to explore and enjoy.

Greenbanks

Coptiviney, nr. Ellesmere, Shropshire SY12 0ND

Tel: 01691 623420   Fax: 01691 623420
wilson.clarke@ukonline.co.uk

Christopher & Tanda Wilson-Clarke

All is comfort and elegance in Tanda and Christopher's pretty, mellow red-brick Victorian home, built in 1865 for a local wine merchant. Relax in the large, sunny, pale yellow-walled, south-facing drawing room. Linger over a hearty breakfast at the long table in the charming pink dining room. A cheery rocking horse greets you outside the bright bedrooms and light pours in through floor-to-ceiling windows. Soft carpets, brass beds, gorgeous views... and a wonderful shower that American visitors tell Tanda is the best they've found this side of the Atlantic.

Rooms:
1 twin/double and 1 twin,
both en suite.
Price:
£32 p.p. Single supp. £10.
Meals:
Dinner, by arrangement.
Closed:
Christmas.

From M6, take M54, then A5 to Shrewsbury. At first r'bout, right for Ellesmere. There, A528 for Shrewsbury at r'bout. 10 yds on, left into Swan Hill. 1 mile on, left onto 'No Through Road'. 0.5 mile on, left over cattle grid.

The Old Priory

Dunster, Somerset TA24 6RY

Tel: 01643 821540

Jane Forshaw

Ancient, rambling, beamed and flagstoned, with sunshine filtering through medieval windows, Jane's 12th-century home is as much a haven for reflection and good company today as it was to the monastic community who once lived here. She has stamped her own style on the priory, with funky Venetian-red walls in the low-ceilinged, time-worn living room with its magnificent stone 14th-century fireplace and, in one bedroom, decoratively painted wardrobe doors. The big bedroom is unforgettable – undulating oaken floor and four-poster – and deeply authentic. A rare place.

JANE FORSHAW'S BEWITCHING SECRET WALLED GARDEN in the beautiful little west Somerset town of Dunster is a wonderfully personal creation. You'll discover a bounteous blend of formal touches with shrubs, small trees and climbers which are allowed to express themselves freely. The garden perfectly complements her ancient priory home... a place of reflection, seclusion and peace. A tall mimosa greets you at the little gate on a lane overlooked by the Castle, mature espaliered fruit trees line the garden path and then comes Jane's most formal touch, the square, knee-high hedged box garden. The shrubs for this were rescued from the Castle's 'Dream Garden' when the National Trust abandoned it because they thought it would be too labour-consuming to maintain. Jane piled as many of the uprooted shrubs as she could into the back of a van, heeled them into some empty land and later arranged them into their present design. Informally planted herbaceous borders and a little lawn in front of the house complete the picture. Through an archway you wander into the church grounds with stunning long beds which Jane helps maintain. When the writer Simon Jenkins drew up his list of the best churches in England, Dunster received star billing and the grounds did even better. He described it as the most delightful church garden in England... see if you agree.

Rooms:
1 ground-floor twin, 1 double, both with private showers; 1 twin and 1 four-poster, both en suite (bath).
Price:
£22.50-£32.50 p.p. Single supp. by arrangement.
Meals:
Available locally.
Closed:
Christmas.

Turn off A39 into village of Dunster, right at blue sign 'unsuitable for goods vehicles'. Follow until church. House is adjoined.

LESLEY'S GARDEN WAS CREATED 30 YEARS AGO with deep herbaceous borders around the walled back garden, a welcoming front garden and little orchard cleverly planted so that the fruits of the trees ripen in succession. Tidy trees give height in the open back garden: a deep purple lilac, crab apple and quince... and a tiny, gnarled plum tree which perfectly frames one of the downstairs windows. In one corner stands a wide pergola smothered with rambling roses and, in winter, the sweetest scents from lonicera fragrantissima. Robert's zany yew topiary is great fun, adding very unusual touches. The position couldn't be more delightful, with a mysterious, high-hedged avenue which leads up from one side of the house to the robust village church with its 1510 tower and, if you're lucky, a peal from the 1606 bells. Lesley has planted herbs in front of the house so that she can reach out to pluck bay, rosemary and other herbs for meals. A pretty magnolia stellata and vigorous white roses which ramble up the front of the house and around one of the bedroom windows give a sparkling welcome in their season. Prevailing south westerly winds usually blanket sounds from the nearby M5, close enough to Causeway Cottage for those wanting to break a journey for a good night's sleep in a very special place.

Rooms:
1 twin, en suite (bath);
1 double, en suite (shower).
Price:
£25-£28 p.p. Single supp.
by arrangement.
Meals:
Supper or dinner by arrangement.
Closed:
Christmas.

Exit M5 at junc. 26 and take West Buckland road for 0.75 miles. First left just before Stone garage. Bear right; 3rd house at end of lane, below church.

If you have been to Johannesburg, you may know their old Bay Tree Restaurant. Robert is a South African and as easy and interesting as they so often are. Lesley now cooks wonderful meals at the cottage and runs cookery courses, too. It's a delicious place; a perfect Somerset cottage with lovely views – an added bonus comes when the church tower above is floodlit at night. The interior is utterly in keeping: pine, coir carpets, straw table mats, wooden beams on the ceilings and a warm sense of fun in a delightful family home. Children over 10 welcome.

Causeway Cottage

West Buckland, Wellington, Somerset TA21 9JZ

Tel: 01823 663458 Fax: 01823 663458
orrs@westbuckland.freeserve.co.uk
members.tripod.com/~causeway_cottage/causeway.htm

Lesley & Robert Orr

Gatchells

Angersleigh, Taunton, Somerset TA3 7SY

Tel: 01823 421580
gatchells@somerweb.co.uk

Mandy Watts

Map No: 1

TRUNDLE DOWN THE LONG FARM TRACK past rich fields and, at the final twist of the drive, a secluded, sturdy thatched home comes into view, wrapped in the leaf and colour of the beautifully tended cottage garden. This, with its panoramic views across fields and hills, was already in good shape when Mandy and Mike arrived in 1991 and they have only made minor changes, enhancing the basic layout they inherited. The one-acre garden has strong bones with low stone walls, rockery beds, a paved terrace with Lady's Mantle peeping through the cracks, a meticulously cared-for, near-formal vegetable and fruit garden and a dappled orchard which they are currently re-planting. Albertine roses bring subtle scent and colour to the front of the house and Mandy adores traditional favourites including iris, showy oriental poppies, fine old roses and, a speciality of hers, stately lupins, all of which she weaves into colourful displays. But she also takes a keen interest in finding new and unusual plants, and there's nothing she enjoys more than chatting about gardens with visitors. One of her recent projects is the a turfed spring garden in the little spinney opposite the front of the house.

Built in 1420 and later lived in by Thomas Gatchell, this is one of the oldest houses in the area. The rooms are immaculate and dramatic. A huge inglenook fireplace with a vast beam houses a wood-burning stove and dominates the guest sitting room. Breakfast is served in the large kitchen or in the sunny conservatory overlooking a swimming pool where you can enjoy a summer splash. Sloping ceilings, soaring beams and pale walls in the bedrooms, and, if you have the main bedroom, don't miss the rings etched in the 17th century on the beams – they ward off evil spirits, so you should sleep soundly.

Rooms:
1 double/family room,
1 twin/double, both en suite
(bath/shower); 1 double,
with private bathroom.
Price:
£21-£27 p.p. Family room for
2 people £50.
Single occ. £30-£35.
Meals:
Dinner £12-£13.50 p.p.
Closed:
Occasionally.

From Trull, just south of
Taunton, take right turn marked
Angersleigh into Dipford Rd.
Follow for 2 miles. Gatchells
marked on right. Take country
track to cottage at end.

DRIVE DOWN TREE-CANOPIED LANES to discover this pretty thatched cottage tucked neatly above a gentle wooded valley. The garden is barely glimpsed at first... and then comes the sight of a simply breathtaking traditional cottage garden with glorious views over an intimate corner of Somerset countryside. Colvin and Pam, escapees from suburbia, have transformed a neglected patch of land into every visitor's vision of the English cottage garden. A little well and a stretch of lawn in front of the house, flower and vegetable-packed terraces that entice you to explore, and colour and life everywhere. Beyond lies the couple's cleverly planted young arboretum, already starting to flesh out. All the favourites are found around the cottage, blowsy oriental poppies including a display of the wickedly smoky Patty's Plum, tall tree lupins, peonies, old roses, tulips, foxgloves and many unusual plants, too; Pam can never resist rarities on her plant-hunting expeditions at local stalls and shows. Everything in the garden is informal, pretty and traditional, making the grounds a magnet for garden lovers from miles around on charity open days. In the spring, wild flowers are encouraged. In summer, the irregularly-shaped beds and borders burst with colour and the autumn sees a glorious display of leaf tints within and without the garden. Overseas visitors are often in raptures; Japanese enthusiasts, particularly, click through reels of film. Some enthusiastic regulars even insist on forming weeding parties, spending their days on hands and knees among the displays.

Rooms:
1 double with private bathroom;
1 single, sharing private bathroom
if in same party; 1 family room,
en suite (bath).
Price:
£15-£17 p.p. Single occ. £24.
Meals:
Dinner, 2 courses £10 p.p.,
3 courses £12 p.p.
Closed:
Never.

From Taunton, south on B3170, or,
from A303/A30, north on B3170. Turn
for Churchinford and follow signs up
Church Road for Stapley.

The Parrys describe their cottage as "happy" and they take genuine pleasure in sharing it. This is a magical and peaceful place. Both your hosts are unpretentious, friendly people and Pam dishes up generous portions of good, fresh country food, either in the snug dining room or the airy conservatory. Sit out on the lawn and enjoy one of Pam's real cream teas with home-made scones and jam and lashings of fresh cream... but leave plenty of time before tackling dinner. Simple décor and wonderful value.

Map No: 1

Pear Tree Cottage

Stapley, Churchstanton, Taunton, Somerset TA3 7QA

Tel: 01823 601224   Fax: 01823 601224
colvin.parry@virgin.net

Colvin & Pam Parry

Carpenters

Norton-sub-Hamdon, Somerset TA14 6SN

Tel: 01935 881255 Fax: 01935 881255
mike@cumberlege.esnet.co.uk

Mike & Christabel Cumberlege

Down a sleepy lane in a hamstone village lies a house heavy with local history. A purple wisteria embraces the front door of Carpenters which dates from the 1700s and, until the 1930s, was a carpenter's home; the sunny sitting room where guests are welcomed was once his workshop. Christabel places posies from the garden in every room and, in the hall on the day we visited, were deliciously scented daphne cuttings. The house, with soft-coloured walls and carpets, is as immaculately cared for as the garden, with pretty wallpapers in bright bedrooms. Traditional breakfasts with local produce are served in the large kitchen, once used by the village baker.

Map No: 1

CHRISTABEL ONCE WORKED at the plant centre at nearby Montacute House and took a City & Guilds gardening course at Cannington. She and lawnsman/pruner Mike are an excellent team. When they came to Carpenters 11 years ago they inherited a highly-managed, sloping garden enclosed by local hamstone walls with views to Ham and Chiselborough hills. Over the years they have added unusual trees and shrubs to create height and structure; the Catalpa they planted at the start is now large enough to sit beneath on a summer's evening – a perfect place for them to enjoy a glass of Mike's delicious home-made wine. (His half-acre vineyard lies just beyond the garden.) Formally shaped borders have been planted in a loose, informal manner with hardy geraniums, shrub roses and as many violas and other favourites as Christabel can pack in, while striking architectural plants, like acanthus and phormiums, tower above. A climbing frame is festooned with a Sander's white rose, clematis and honeysuckle. Mike keeps the lawns in pristine condition, prunes trees and shrubs and has carved a straggling yew hedge into dramatic, sentinel-like shapes beyond the double borders. From the first spring flowers to the late autumn blaze of acer, this garden holds your interest. The sole exception to Mike and Christabel's strict organic rule is the occasional anti-slug defence of their vegetable garden.

Rooms:
1 twin and 1 single, sharing bathroom.
Price:
£25 p.p.
Meals:
Dinner £18 p.p., packed lunch £5 p.p.
Closed:
24 December-2 January.

From A303 take A356 towards Crewkerne. Disregard left turn to Stoke-sub-Hamdon and continue 1 mile to cross roads. Left into Norton-sub-Hamdon and first right into Higher St. Drive up to bend and straight ahead through Carpenters gateway by small greenhouse.

AN EXCITING YOUNG GARDEN packed with detail. This is an intricately planted
30 x 60 metre area created over the past five years and now open to admiring NGS
visitors. The complex plan was drawn by a professional and Alison and Brian have
successfully turned drawings into reality in the new garden bounded by the
farmhouse, a little river and fields. Successions of small seating areas are linked by
walks with different aspects, visual surprises and the sound of running water from
the stream that Brian made with old stones found on the farm. It rises in a swirl
pool and gurgles under bridges, over miniature waterfalls and through a lily pond
and bog garden where water-lovers like Primula Candelabra flourish. Alison loves
traditional plant favourites like iris, her 25 varieties of delphinium, rose, clematis,
penstemon and 40 varieties of dahlia which she lifts and stores each winter in the
adjoining mill. Arches gleam with climbing roses and there are eye-catching details
like the horseshoe of iceberg roses. Colour is themed subtly with red/yellow/
blue/white, pink/mauve/purple and blue/gold. This is a garden where you can
admire colour and detail on any day, from the initial flush of iris to autumn's
golden leaf displays.

Map No: 1

Gants Mill

Bruton, Somerset BA10 0DB

Tel: 01749 812393
shingler@gantsmill.co.uk
www.gantsmill.co.uk

Alison & Brian Shingler

In Victorian times the resident miller brought up his family of 13 children here – the place had to be extended for the task. Brian has a fine photograph of the bearded patriarch and brood. Today you can breakfast at their original table or, on sunnier days, enjoy the wisteria-clad conservatory with the present-day family's pet dogs and cats. Bedrooms are functional but large, with brass bedheads and dark wood furniture, flower prints and displays of old plates. Do ask Brian for a tour of the adjoining watermill where he grinds grain for his sheep and keeps a small museum.

Rooms:
1 family, en suite (shower);
1 double, private bathroom.
Price:
£25 p.p.
Meals:
Not available.
Closed:
21 December-2 January.

Signed off the A359, half a mile south-west of Bruton.

SWEEPING LAWNS, MATURE TREES, a 14th-century church below, a south-facing suntrap terrace, a formal rose garden, pools and curious topiary... Pennard House is one of those dreamy landscape gardens straight from the pages of P. G. Wodehouse. All seems serene, free and easy – and on a grand scale – yet a huge amount of time and hard work has gone into developing and restoring the grounds of Susie's family's house. Shady laurels and yews were the dominant feature until the couple launched a clearance and restoration campaign after taking advice from expert friends. Pennard House has, in fact, two gardens within a garden, divided by a little lane. There are the open, sunny lawns of the house garden and, across the road, a second garden with clipped hedges, a formal rose garden and an inviting spring-fed Victorian swimming pool which in turn feeds a series of ponds below. Don't miss the wacky topiary cottage, rabbit and other creatures which the gardener has created over the years. Susie always has some new project afoot – a recent success was ripping out cotoneaster below the terrace and replacing it with a pretty, formally-planted combination of rosemary, roses and lavender. Drag chairs onto the lawn and curl up with a book, swim in the crystal clear water of the pool, or simply stroll among the colour, the scents and the blooms.

Map No: 1

Pennard House

East Pennard, Shepton Mallet, Somerset BA4 6TP

Tel: 01749 860266   Fax: 01749 860266
m.dearden@ukonline.co.uk   www.sawdays.co.uk

Martin & Susie Dearden

One of the grandest houses in this book, Pennard has been in Susie's family since the 17th century – the cellars date from then. The superstructure is stately, lofty Georgian, but the Deardens are delightfully unstuffy and welcoming. Guests have the run of the library, formal drawing room, billiards room and six acres of garden with a pool. Or walk in 300 acres of cider orchards, meadows and woods. Martin deals in antiques; Susie was born and brought up here and is familiar with all there is to do and see in the area. It is warm and civilised with plain, properly unhotelly bedrooms.

Rooms:
1 double and 1 twin,
both en suite (shower/bath);
1 double/twin with private bathroom;
1 single with private bathroom.
Price:
From £30 p.p. Single occ.
by arrangement.
Meals:
Available locally.
Closed:
Christmas.

South on A37 from Shepton Mallet, through Pylle and next right to East Pennard. Pass church to T-junction at very top. House on left.

PHOEBE HAS CREATED A GLORIOUSLY OPEN, natural garden around her gorgeous house on a Somerset hillside, 600 feet above sea level. The views are ravishing, with romantic Glastonbury Tor to the west and the southern folds of the Mendip hills to the north. The main garden is about an acre but it spills over into another couple of informal acres and home paddocks beyond. There's a pond, too, first mentioned in the 10th century, where you may spot a Little Grebe at play, one of the oldest recorded wells in Somerset and you are on the ancient pilgrim route from Ditcheat to Glastonbury. Phoebe isn't one for fussy borders and the most formal feature is the garden to the west, planted to encourage the eye to follow the path which draws you to the sight of the Tor. She tried to make a row of pleached lime in front of the house, but greedy racehorses have created an avenue instead by chomping side branches! A cloud of catmint greets you at the front door and, around the corner, she has done wonders with the cobbled courtyard. Phoebe is a devoted container gardener. She skilfully plants potted lilies among perennial herbaceous plants to give her borders added interest and the courtyard's edges, with their free-growing euphorbias, have a glorious collection of plants in large pots which she can move as the mood suits her. A blissful place and a garden which makes the very most of its greatest asset – those views.

Rooms:
1 double, en suite; 1 double suite & 3 singles, sharing private bathroom; 1 double suite.
Price:
Suites £140 per night.
Other rooms £45-£65 p.p.
Meals:
Dinner £25 p.p. Lunch £17.50 p.p.
Closed:
Never.

From Wells, A39 to Glastonbury. Left at North Wootton sign. Follow signs for West Pennard. At T-junction right onto A361. After 400m, first left. Through tunnel of trees, drive on left.

A more exquisite house would be hard to find. Phoebe, a shepherd, sought the perfect home: she found it. The antique beds have handmade mattresses, and fat pillows and in the barn you have luxurious privacy. The indoor swimming pool gives on to the spectacular view, through a Gothic, arched window. It's all magnificent. Babies and children over 12 welcome.

Map No: 1

Pennard Hill Farm

Stickleball Hill, East Pennard, Shepton Mallet, Somerset BA4 6UG

Tel: 01749 890221   Fax: 01749 890665

Phoebe Judah

Beryl

Wells, Somerset BA5 3JP

Tel: 01749 678738   Fax: 01749 670508
stay@beryl-wells.co.uk   www.beryl-wells.co.uk

Eddie & Holly Nowell

A lofty, mullioned, low-windowed home – light and bright, devoid of Victorian gloom. They have filled it with a fine collection of antiques and every bedroom has a talking point... a four-poster here, a time-worn baby's cot there. The flowery top-floor rooms in the attic have a Gothic Revival feel with arched doorways; one first-floor room has a stunning old bath, sumptuously clad in mahogany and with its very own tiny staircase. Candelit dinners carefully prepared by Holly, breakfasts in the sunny dining room, tea in the richly elegant drawing room – all this and the wonders of Wells just below.

Map No: 1

HOLLY SAYS 'BERYL' MEANS a meeting of hills; Eddie has his own description: "a precious gem in a perfect setting". Beryl is a small, early-Victorian mansion with south-facing grounds gazing down to dreamy Wells Cathedral. Eddie, one of the city's most colourful characters, runs an antique shop in the Market Place and, in season, wears a buttonhole of his favourite rambling rose, American Pillar. He is a devoted gardener who has put in countless hours to restore the grounds from an overgrown shambles to their original Victorian splendour. A broad terrace leads to open lawns, a formal staircase and a wildlife pool, while avenues draw the eye towards the views. The striking steel armillary sphere is a memorial to their son Julius, who loved this large garden. Beyond lies well-tended woodland – Eddie has planted more than 4,000 trees and strewn wild daffodils among them – and Beryl's most ravishing feature, the very large walled garden. There are garden 'rooms' and deep, generously planted borders intersected by paths edged by catmint and low box hedges. A cutting bed provides a rich supply of flowers for the house and the vegetable beds will supply your plate. Eddie collects hollies as a tribute to his wife's name and he celebrated her 50th birthday by planting 50 white hydrangeas. Victorian garden elegance, profusions of flowers, magical woodland walks... no wonder Beryl's charity open days are always such a celebration.

Rooms:
2 four-posters, 3 doubles and 3 twins, all en suite (bath/shower).
Price:
Double occ. £32.50-£47.50 p.p.
Single occ £50-£65.
Meals:
Dinner £22.50 p.p.
Closed:
Christmas.

Leave Wells on Radstock Rd B3139, follow 'H' sign for hospital and The Horringtons. Left into Hawkers Lane opp. garage. Follow lane to top and sign 'Beryl'.

Hollytree Cottage

Laverton, Somerset BA3 6QZ

Tel: 01373 830786   Fax: 01373 830786

Julia Naismith

*Meandering lanes lead you to this 17th-century cottage –
quintessentially English with roses round the door, a grandfather
clock in the hall and an air of genteel tranquillity. Julia has updated
the cottage charm with Regency mahogany in the inglenook dining
room and sumptuous sofas in the sitting room. Bedrooms have long
views over farmland and undulating countryside; behind is a
conservatory and the sloping, south-facing garden. Do ask your
hostess about Bath (just 20 minutes away) – she worked in the
Holburne Museum and knows the city well.*

TWENTY YEARS OF trial and error have gone into creating this cottage garden which slopes gently down from the house to fields below and which complements the house perfectly. It has everything you could want in an open, informal country garden. Very good trees and shrubs including a tamarisk, a white-flowering Amelanchier and a soft pink Magnolia stellata have been introduced over the years. A tall laburnum flowers profusely in season and Julia's collection of prunus have been carefully planted so that they flower in succession in spring time. A series of irregular beds have been dug and planted with skill and flair, providing colour and interest from a wide variety of good plants. Julia is a keen member of her local horticultural society and buys many treasures at their plant sales, including clematis from the late Betty Risdon who ran the famous Rode Bird Gardens nearby and who was a leading member of the Clematis Society. Fish swim in the little pond, surrounded by water-loving plants and for fresh vegetables and fruit, there is an immaculate kitchen garden edged with recycled railway sleepers. The small conservatory is absolutely packed with the more tender plants, a perfect spot to sit and enjoy the colour and interest outside. The position is delightful and the garden has been designed to make the most of its glorious views.

Rooms:
1 double/family room
(1 single let to same party),
1 twin & 1 single, all en suite
(shower).
Price:
£25-£30 p.p. Reduction for
longer stays.
Meals:
Available locally.
Closed:
Never.

From Bath or Warminster take A36 to Woolverton. Opposite Red Lion pub take Laverton turning. 1 mile to cross-roads and continue toward Faulkland/ Wellow (signposted) downhill 80 yards. House on left.

Lavenham Priory

Water Street, Lavenham, Sudbury, Suffolk CO10 9RW

Tel: 01787 247404   Fax: 01787 248472

mail@lavenhampriory.co.uk   www.lavenhampriory.co.uk

Tim & Gilli Pitt

A LOVELY, RAMBLING HOUSE and a large garden with field views that complement the superb setting of this famously beautiful Suffolk town; its streets of half-timbered buildings and painted exteriors are most striking. Since they moved here in the mid-1990s, Gilli and Tim have worked creatively to transform the four acres stretching back behind their gorgeous home from a long, largely open stretch of land into a place of interest and contrasts. Gilli looks after colour, flowers and the details, Tim the broader picture. One very useful feature they have inherited is a walnut grove, planted by the previous owners to one side of the grounds. It now gives a fine crop, alongside fruit from pear and apple trees. Tim's efforts have been Herculean; he has laid a staggering quarter mile of hedges, mostly of hawthorn, to divide the grounds into compartments and planted many trees, including black poplar, as part of a national effort to bring back this species. The new herb garden in the courtyard behind the house is a delightful touch: culinary, medicinal and scented beds are divided by laid flintstones into a neat, bountiful design. Beyond, open lawns lead past the orchard and a well tended kitchen garden to a little wildflower meadow with, to one side, a cooling ash grove. There's a wildlife pond which is home to majestic bulrushes and a sanctuary for local fauna.

An impressive, beautifully decorated and furnished Grade I-listed house dating from the 13th century. The hub of this beamed, oak-floored, high-ceilinged family home is the huge stone-flagged Great Hall where you float on a sea of sofas and cushions before the enormous inglenook fireplace. The bright, many-windowed, beam-vaulted bedrooms have handmade mattresses and beds, pure cotton sheets and flowers everywhere; each has its own character. Wonderful details include Elizabethan wall paintings. Children over 10 welcome.

Rooms:
1 double and 1 twin/double, both en suite and 3 four-posters, all en suite (bath & shower).
Price:
£39-£54 p.p. Single occ. £59-£69.
Meals:
Packed lunch and dinner, £27 p.p., by arrangement.
Closed:
Christmas & New Year.

Turn at The Swan onto Water Street then right after 50 yds into private drive to the Priory car park.

A CURVING DRIVE PAST TALL trees leads you to rural peace in a town setting. Passers-by peep through the tall gates in spring to admire snowdrops, aconites and crocuses followed by thousands of daffodils. In summer, tall roses scramble up the porticoed façade of the de la Rue's elegant home set among lawns with an imposing flagpole, walled gardens and borders. A dozen box balls add a formal flourish to the sunny terrace. Within the Georgian walled area you'll find a formal paved rose garden with roses growing between flagstones. Walk through a rose-covered arch past a fruiting fig to the large kitchen garden with its immaculate little box hedges leading you along the paths. A complete change of mood comes at the far end of the main lawn, with a superb meadow on a gentle slope and woodland. This is a Country Wildlife site with Southern Marsh orchids and a profusion of other wild flowers. More than 100 species have been recorded, from spring's meadow saxifrage and cuckoo flowers to summer's carpets of ladies' bedstraw and the purples and whites of knapweed and yarrow. A grass path follows the meadow's perimeter and goes through the adjoining woodland with two ponds. Bird-lovers will be in their element: spotted flycatchers, mistle thrush, song thrush, both great spotted and green woodpeckers. A garden that perfectly combines the formal and informal with the natural beauty of an all-too-rare plot of uncultivated, flower-filled grassland.

Map No: 2

Melton Hall

Woodbridge, Suffolk IP12 1PF

Tel: 01394 388138   Fax: 01394 388982

Mrs Lucinda de la Rue

A beautifully proportioned house in seven and a half acres of gardens, meadows and woodland. Cindy is energetic, with enough enthusiasm for her young family and her guests. Flagstoned hall, a large oak table in a striking burgundy dining room and a fine sitting room with French windows. The bedrooms are well furnished and have maps, books, radio, fresh flowers and garden views; one has a wrought-iron four-poster with beautiful embroidered linen.

Rooms:
1 double room, and 1 single (with basin) sharing adjacent bathroom; 1 double, en suite (bath).
Price:
Double from £27p.p.; single £20. Fri & Sat £2 p.p. extra.
Meals:
Dinner £12.50-£16 p.p., by arrangement. B.Y.O. wine. Lunch & packed lunch available on request.
Closed:
Never.

From A12 Woodbridge by pass, exit at roundabout signed Orford and Melton. Follow for 1 mile to lights; there, turn right and house is immediately on right.

DRIVE DOWN THE SLEEPY LANE through waving crop fields to find the secluded peace of the garden that has been developing over the past 20 years. The house has been in the family for 150 years and where once there were three full-time gardeners to tend the large grounds, today Teena and Richard manage it with the help of one part-timer. The bones are glorious: fine walls, a backdrop of lofty, mature trees, views to Suffolk farmland, a moat in front of the house where water lilies prosper, a large pond overhung with flowering shrubs. Teena has embellished the grounds with great style; planting, weaving a tapestry of new features and always keeping labour-saving in mind. Where once there were time-consuming displays of annuals there are now shrubs and perennials. Hyacinths and daffodils bloom in profusion by the moat in spring-time, and a little copse at one end is a mass of snowdrops. Summer sees one of Teena's best touches – the arched rose walk neatly underplanted with box balls – come into its own; she loves topiary. Sit outside on the lavender-scented patio and enjoy an evening drink, gaze down from the little bridge over the moat and watch the fish play, and walk among the many specimen trees Richard has planted in the dappled grassy area between lane and moat. Throughout, the Freelands have introduced the many colours of maturing shrubs, trees and winding borders, in golds, coppers and every shade of green.

Map No: 2

The Elms

Toft Monks, Beccles, Suffolk NR34 0EJ

Tel: 01502 677380   Fax: 01502 677362
richardfreeland@btconnect.com
www.sawdays.co.uk

Richard & Teena Freeland

*Flemish flax weavers used to wash the flax in the
moat and dry it in the magnificent barn.
Grade II*-listed, red-brick and mellow, the house has
a grand scale: soaring ceilings, handsome fireplaces,
huge sash windows, cast-iron baths, good, large, beds.
It's full of light, and parquet floors; chandelier,
balustrade and frescos add grandeur. Guests have
their own sitting room. Evenings here are heavenly –
a drink on the terrace, dinner, then a wander
through the garden or even a game of tennis.
Richard and Teena are delightful.*

Rooms:
1 double with private bathroom;
1 twin, en suite (bath).
Price:
£35 p.p. Single supp. £10.
Meals:
Dinner from £25 p.p.,
by arrangement.
Closed:
Occasionally.

Take A143 Yarmouth/Beccles road. In
Toft Monks take Post Office Rd
(opposite Toft Lion pub) for 0.4
miles to T-junc. Right down Aldeby
Rd for 0.1 mile, fork right and house
is on right, 0.2 miles on.

MARY'S GARDEN IS AS LAID-BACK as its owner and her home. All is informal and cottagey and in perfect harmony with this old Sussex farmhouse on the little Chidham peninsula. Half an acre set in farmland, it has evolved over the past 30 years. Its dominating feature, on the main lawn behind the house, is the Catalpa tree which Mary planted 25 years ago and which now stretches its loose-limbed branches in a handsome umbrella of pale green leaves. Around the house, borders are piled high with shrubs and herbaceous plants, including blue agapanthus and stately acanthus, while climbers reach up the façade. Herringbone brick paths lead you past banks of roses and vigorous shrubs from one area to the next. In one corner there is a circular mini-garden edged with grass, shrubs, a surround of brick and stone and, above, the shady embrace of a walnut tree. Mary's latest project is an elaborate knot garden, with a pattern of curves made from low-cut box hedges. Her cats laze in the little grove of silver birch with its dappled shade, the sound of birdsong is everywhere and the sea breezes are soft. Perfect peace.

Easton House

Chidham Lane, Chidham, Chichester, Sussex
PO18 8TF

Tel: 01243 572514   Fax: 01243 573084
eastonhouse@chidhamfsnet.co.uk

Mary Hartley

*Lots of beams, charming bedrooms, a cosily
cluttered drawing room with a Bechstein piano
and comfortable armchairs: this is a haven for
musicians – and cat-lovers. It has the feel of a well-
loved and lived-in family home; Mary has lived here
for 30 years. The house looks out over Chidham
harbour "five minutes walk from the water's edge"
and is surrounded by great walking and bird-
watching country. A lovely setting for a
delightful house.*

Rooms:
1 twin and 1 double with shared
bathroom; 1 double with private
bathroom.
Price:
From £21 p.p.
Meals:
Excellent pub in village.
Closed:
Christmas.

From Chichester, head for
Portsmouth. Pass Tesco on right. 3rd
exit off r'bout, to Bosham &
Fishbourne. Follow A259 for 4 miles,
pass Saab garage on right. Next left
into Chidham Lane. House last on
left, 1 mile down.

Amberfold

Heyshott, Midhurst, Sussex GU29 0DA

Tel: 01730 812385   Fax: 01730 812842
www.sawdays.co.uk

Alex & Annabelle Costaras

A secret hideaway in the woods, Amberfold isn't just a B&B but a retreat, perfect for a pair of independent nature-lovers. You have your own lavishly stocked fridge (replenished daily) – there's enough for a copious breakfast with plenty to spare for a picnic lunch as well.
The rooms are pristine and decorated in a simple country house style, you have your own front door and terrace, and there are miles of beautiful, unspoilt woodlands to explore right on the doorstep. Don't jump out of your skin if a deer comes to your window to investigate!

Map No: 2

ANNABELLE'S PRETTY, TERRACED COTTAGE GARDEN is alive with the sound of birdsong and avian chatter – daughters Natalie and Katie have their own home-bred cockatiels, finches, budgies and tiny Japanese quail. The woodland-surrounded garden took on its current form in the 1950s when the cottages were converted into a single home – until then, the garden had been on a steep slope. In a major re-design, the slope was transformed into three terraces with central York stone steps from the front door to a rustic garden gate that gives onto adjoining acres of completely unspoilt woodland. Annabelle believes in labour-intensive gardening – and how! Her greenhouse is always on the go, whatever the season. Each year she grows thousands of bedding plants for her ever-widening borders; she tends hanging baskets and floral tubs and waters and nurtures her floral 'babies' to maturity, so that by mid-summer there is masses of colour everywhere. Her kitchen garden around the corner is, as you'd expect, just as productive as her beds and borders. You'll be charmed by a delightful example of inspired garden architecture in the vine-covered child's playhouse. Alexander created this on a brick base with half-timbering to match the timber-framed main house. Walk the woods, relax on one of the sunny terraces – you are immersed in total peace.

Rooms:
2 studios, both doubles with shower and wc.
Price:
From £25 p.p. Single supp. from £10.
Meals:
Local pubs within walking distance.
Closed:
Never.

From Midhurst, A286 towards Chichester. After Royal Oak pub on left, Greyhound on right, go 0.5 miles, left to Graffham and Heyshott. On for 2 miles, do not turn off, look for white posts and house sign on left.

Little Orchard House

West Street, Rye, Sussex TN31 7ES   Tel: 01797 223831   Fax: 01797 2238.

Sara Brinkhurst

Map No: 2

NOT A HINT OF THE FEAST to come as you climb the steep, narrow, richly atmospheric little cobbled street which leads to Sara's magical home in hauntingly beautiful Rye. But just step outside the back door and you're in another, totally unexpected world. Wind bells chime, paths duck, dive and snake around hidden corners, a few steps lead from one enclosed area to the next. A little sea monster 'swims' across a lawn, its coils rising and falling among the grass. It has taken Sara 10 years to weave this secret garden tapestry from a large, somewhat unprepossessing back garden and transform it into a half acre of romantically informal areas, each with a character of its own and each hidden from the next. Everything here speaks of a passion for gardening and nature. Her pond and herb garden has colour-themed planting, with low, manicured box hedges and thriving espaliered pears. A trellis groans with clematis and for utter peace and contemplation, seek out the little arbour and rest on the seat, leaning back against an old, carved wooden panel beneath the shelter of a golden hop. Just by you a cobbled water feature tinkles while seagulls wheel and cry overhead. Gaze up at the all-seeing watchtower with its weather vane, admire the colour and interest of the well-planted beds and borders and note those little details and personal touches Sara has added, like the cartwheel cleverly placed behind the rockery. No wonder guests love this garden.

"Teddy bears inside, hedgehogs outside and a really excellent cat". This most welcoming, rule-free townhouse in history-laden Rye also has fine antiques, masses of books and paintings, occasional groups of amateur dramatists in the big and otherwise quiet garden, a Smugglers' Watchtower and a small library for rainy days. Sara is lively, attentive and fun and will give you big organic/ free-range breakfasts.
Children over 12 welcome.

Rooms:
2 four-posters, both en suite (1 shower, 1 bath/shower).
Price:
£32-£45 p.p. Single occ. £45-£65.
Meals:
Available locally.
Closed:
Never.

From A268 or A259, follow one-way system to town centre, through Landgate Arch, into High Street. West Street is third turning on left. House is halfway up on left. Parking available.

The Old Manor House

Halford, Shipston-on-Stour, Warwickshire CV36 5BT

Tel: 01789 740264   Fax: 01789 740609   wpusey@st-philips.co.uk

Jane & William Pusey

Map No: 2

ROSE-LOVERS – NO, ALL GARDEN LOVERS, but rosarians in particular – will adore the garden Jane and William have created over the past five years. With a background of high mature trees and a sloping three acres, they have built a series of loosely, rather than formally, linked areas. They have added new beech and yew hedges, planted vigorously and sympathetically and made a garden that sits beautifully with their lovely old home. Old roses rule above all, climbing up walls, rambling over pergolas and arches, softening hard corners and, in a final flourish, scenting and colouring a delightful rose avenue. There is a blend of the stiffer hybrid teas, which Jane inherited and can't find the heart to remove, and a riot of treasures from sources including Peter Beales. At the time of writing, Jane was sending vigorous climbers like Kiftsgate rocketing up the trees in the orchard. It will be gorgeous, but there is much, much more: cleverly planted borders, a delicious herb garden where sage, fennel, thyme and others rub shoulder, delightful colour-theming in flower beds bursting with good plants and so many details as well as a glorious overall feel to enjoy. William has strong ideas about design, Jane has strong ideas about plants and planting. Between them, they have made the very best of the lay of their three acres and their infectious love of plants and garden design.

You'll be in your element if you fish or play tennis, for you can do both from the beautiful gardens that slope gently down to the River Stour. Jane, a Cordon Bleu cook, runs her 16th- and 17th-century house with huge energy and friendliness. A pretty blue twin bedroom and a single room are in a self-contained room with its own large, elegant drawing and dining room; it's seductively easy to relax here. The A-shaped double, with ancient beams and oak furniture, is in the main part of the house; it has a lovely bathroom and shares the drawing and dining rooms.

Rooms:
1 double, 1 twin, both with private bathroom; 1 single (let only to same party as twin), private bathroom.
Price:
From £28 p.p. Single supp. £5.
Meals:
Dinner, by arrangement.
Closed:
Occasionally.

From Stratford, follow A422 for 4 miles towards Banbury. Turn right at r'bout onto A429 for Halford. In village, take first right. House with black and white timbers straight ahead.

THE POSITION IS RAVISHING, on an open village green with orchards beyond. And, above, the final thrust of the Cotswold edge. This is the English village of everyone's dreams. Gail's Victorian home, covered with Virginia creeper and facing the green, is fronted by a bold row of sculpted topiary and a little garden with a collection of cottagey flowers and a magnolia tree to set off the neat façade. The drive to the side has its very own tribute to the world-famous gardens at nearby Hidcote... a flourishing row of Hidcote blue lavender. Canadian-born Gail inherited the garden much as it is today, with its open, sunny back garden, orchard and little walled garden. Today she is devotedly helped in the grounds by gardener Sue Upstone. Gail takes particular pleasure in her orchard of apple and pear trees and the very productive, immaculately kept vegetable garden which provides fresh produce for the house. A keen cook, she has added a little herb garden at the foot of one of the walls where she picks fresh herbs for her meals. American visitors love the flowers, and Japanese guests are totally enthralled by the vigorous rhubarb – most have never seen it before. Enjoy afternoon tea in the front garden and enjoy the lovely setting and views.

Winton House

The Green, Upper Quinton,
Stratford-upon-Avon, Warwickshire CV37 8SX

Tel: 01789 720500
gail@wintonhouse.com
www.wintonhouse.com

Mrs Gail Lyon

There are log fires to warm your enthusiasm for a good walk on the Heart of England Way. The views stretch on to folklore-rich Meon Hill and if the stories of local witchcraft fail to spark your imagination, there is every chance your bed will inspire you. The Angel Room has a pine box bed and a medieval frieze of flying angels. The two other rooms have romantic four-posters with handmade quilts. Healthy and delicious menus – 'Winton House Specials' – change daily and make imaginative use of organic fruit from the orchard.

Rooms:
2 doubles, en suite; 1 twin/family room, with private bathroom.
Price:
From £28 p.p.
Meals:
Available locally.
Closed:
Never.

From Stratford A3400, right on B4632. 6 miles on, left into Upper Quinton. 0.5 miles on left.

The Crofts Farm

Banbury Road, Stratford-upon-Avon, Warwickshire CV37 7NF

Tel: 01789 292159
edstell@croftsfarm.freeserve.co.uk

Mrs Stella Davies

There's a sense of escape as you leave behind roads and people and set off down the farm's track. The 1750s gentleman farmer's house is red-brick Georgian, so typical of this area – rooms are beautifully proportioned, as you'd expect, and floor-to-ceiling windows add sunny elegance. The bright hall has a particularly delicate staircase teetering above it and at the top you find magnificent oak floors. One of the bedrooms is pale yellow with bold printed curtains and another has a perfect view of the rose garden below. Stella and Eddie are smashing and have a lively sense of humour. Children over 12 welcome.

Map No: 2

STELLA DOES FLOWERS AND DESIGN and Eddie is the hard landscaping man; between them they have transformed the grounds around their working 280-acre farm. Stella is a born colourist, cleverly theming areas in shades of pinks and white, blue and white and, in one tiny corner, purples; the vibrant Knautia Macedonia sets off the wonderfully hazy beauty of a Smoke Plant (cotinus). A carefully thought-out rose garden fronts the house and has four box-edged formal beds crammed with good roses – some stiff and upright, others blowsy and floppy. It's hard to believe that until recently this was the old grass tennis court. Elsewhere, Stella has made a series of gardens-within-a garden; a hot, orange-painted corner here, a woodland there where wild flowers grow in profusion. Eddie has moved entire hedges of beech and box to complement the drama of her planting. Yew hedges lead to an elegant white-painted iron fence and gate which gives onto the fields beyond, so you have interest within and without. Most of the garden has been re-worked over the past three years and one of the more recent features is a patio paved with reclaimed bricks, a lily pond and a hefty pergola for climbers. A delightful young garden with all-year interest.

Rooms:
1 double and 1 double
and single, both en suite (bath);
1 double with private bathroom.
Price:
From £28 p.p. Single occ. £35.
Meals:
Available locally.
Closed:
November-February.

2 miles south of Stratford-upon-Avon on A422 Banbury road, left at sign to Croft Farm.

Manor Farmhouse

Crudwell, Malmesbury, Wiltshire SN16 9ER

Tel: 01666 577375 Fax: 01666 823523
user785566@aol.com
www.sawdays.co.uk

Helen & Philip Carter

The original granary for Malmesbury Abbey was here; now there is this lovely honey-coloured farmhouse, with Cotswold stone roof with moss and lichen, veg, fruit and flowers from the garden, flagstoned floors and views through old doors and windows. And it is right next to a fine church in a classically pretty village. The views from the surprisingly modern bathroom are inspiring – cattle peacefully grazing in the paddock; the church from another, and little window seats to sit on. It is all delightful and comfortable, too. Helen is a lovely host.

SUNNY MORNINGS MAKE OPEN AIR breakfast in Helen's garden a seductive delight... sit at a table facing west and enjoy the wonderful sight of the 12th-century church just across the tall walls from a garden sparkling with generous planting. You know you're in for a treat from the moment you arrive, passing a dramatic border which leads to the house and planted with carefully tended lime-hating favourites like rhododendron and pieris. The setting, in a conservation area surrounded by trees, is dreamy and Helen has added to the arboreal delights with her own little arboretum, which she began 10 years ago. Today it has matured into a dappled area of peace and calm with specimen trees including the dramatic corkscrew hazel "Harry Lauder's Walking Stick" and a fine whitebeam which she has adorned with the climbing rose "Wedding Day". Helen is a keen flower arranger and has lots of cutting plants in her borders. There's fun in the detail, too: a pergola bearing a Kiftsgate rose, an avenue of rugosa roses, little lavender hedges and her Terracotta Garden with its collection of imaginatively planted containers of all shapes and sizes. Vegetable growers will envy her immaculately tended kitchen garden with its very productive cold frame. A lovely, traditional, south-facing and sunny walled Cotswold garden with interesting plants and a robust charm.

Rooms:
2 doubles, 1 en suite and 1 with private bathroom.
Price:
£25-£30 p.p. Single occ. £25.
Meals:
Dinner, 3 courses, £17.50 p.p. Packed lunch also available, both by arrangement.
Closed:
Christmas & New Year.

A429 Malmesbury to Cirencester. In Crudwell, at Plough, right signed Minety/Oaksey. Straight on, then left between church and tithe barn pillars.

WHAT A NAME – WHAT A GARDEN! Plantsmen traditionally sacrifice design on the altar of collecting, but Antony and Sue combine both in a breathtaking, informal 14-acre plantsman's garden packed with rare shrubs and trees. Born gardeners, the Youngs began here modestly 30 years ago. A defining moment came when Antony abandoned industry for garden design. He now works on commissions, including stately homes here and châteaux in France. In the lower and upper gardens, lawns sweep through displays including 75 different shrub and species roses, daphnes, a dozen different magnolias and a collection of 15 acers in their own glade. A young arboretum has been planted over the past 10 years with radiating avenues of trees including Serbian spruce planted to attract goldcrests. Beyond is a three-acre wild flower meadow with 36 species of native limestone flora. By the house are witty touches of formality with a potager and box garden, but the overall mood is of bountiful informality with glorious details and a ravishing collection of plants. Antony wears his knowledge with engaging lightness and thoroughly enjoys leading guests through the myriad charms of this horticultural masterpiece. Ridleys Cheer opens for the NGS and guests and visitors should leave some room in the car boot – you can buy plants propagated from the garden.

Rooms:
1 double, en suite (bath);
1 double & 1 twin,
sharing bathroom.
Price:
£35 p.p.
Meals:
Packed lunch £8 p.p. Lunch £15 p.p.
Dinner £27.50 p.p. inc. wine.
All by arrangement.
Closed:
Occasionally.

M4 junc. 17. At Chippenham A420 (Bristol). After 9 miles right at The Shoe next to inn. Then 2nd left, then 1st right. You are now in Mountain Bower (no sign). Last house on left with gravel car park opposite.

Ridleys Cheer, in a hamlet approached down meandering lanes populated by suicidal pheasants, was originally a small 18th-century cottage but enlarged in 1989 by the architect, William Bertram, who restored Highgrove. One special addition was the large conservatory where summer guests can breakfast amid plumbago and jasmine. The guestrooms, reached by a separate staircase, are bright, simple and cosy, with pale walls, pretty curtains and antique furniture and the eye is ceaselessly drawn through the small windows to the glories below. Sue, a Cordon Bleu chef, cooks delicious meals served at a mahogany table in the low-ceilinged dining room.

Map No: 2

Ridleys Cheer

Mountain Bower, Chippenham
Wiltshire SN14 7AJ

Tel: 01225 891204 Fax: 01225 891139
antonyoung@aol.com

Sue & Antony Young

The Old Rectory

Luckington, nr. Chippenham, Wiltshire SN14 6PH

Tel: 01666 840556   Fax: 01666 840989

John & Maril Eldred

PURE UNDILUTED COTSWOLDS' CHARM and in a village so perfect that scenes for *Pride and Prejudice* were filmed at the church. You sweep up the curving drive and immediately notice myriad leaf colour in the vibrant borders. John and Maril are hugely modest about what they've achieved in their young garden. They shouldn't be. The two acres around the house sing of the hard work and devotion that they have poured into them. Wisteria drips over the façade and traditional favourites such as sweet peas, delphiniums, tulips and old roses fill the beds opposite. Structural details are interesting, too. The Eldreds have planted a copper and green beech hedge – two coppers, two green, two coppers, etc – which gives impressive contrast and lasting colour; originally fashionable in the '20s and '30s, this sort of planting is enjoying a revival. Over 100 other trees have been planted, too, mostly around the tennis court, and lawns have been nurtured with impressive results. An interesting feature is the recently added fan-shaped pergola, home to climbing roses and other sweet-scented sun seekers. Maril's successes include the kitchen garden, which has a cutting bed for flowers for the house, and John's the planting of a new orchard and the hiding of unsightly power and telephone lines underground.

An architectural oddity – the house has an 1830s façade, yet parts are 14th century. Burning log fires, the smell of coffee wafting from the kitchen and the bustle of family life make you feel immediately at home. Maril has made some bold choices of colour – the strong blue of the dining room has real impact. Bedrooms are big with pretty fabrics and softer colours; the double has a truly huge bathroom. You can play tennis on the all-weather court, try your hand at croquet, swim in the heated pool. Do visit the church, though, it's a step away, through the gate in the 12th-century wall.

Rooms:
1 double, en suite; 1 twin, en suite; 2 bedroom cottage annexe.
Price:
£34 p.p. Single supp. £6.
Meals:
Dinner, by arrangement.
Closed:
Occasionally.

From M4 junc. 17, north for Malmesbury. Take 2nd left and follow road for approx. 4 miles. At Sherston, left onto B4040 for Luckington. 1.5 miles on, leaving Brook End on left, house is on left 0.25 miles before centre of Luckington.

A LARGE, MATURE COUNTRY HOUSE GARDEN which Christopher and Caroline have carefully restored to complement their long, elegant house (18th-century and originally the Home Farm for nearby Dauntsey Park). The stables outside are a reminder of its days as a hunting box for the Duke of Beaufort's hunt. There are glorious lawns, rose-covered dry stone walls and an open, sunny atmosphere. The mature trees are very handsome and include a perfectly shaped decorative sycamore and two lofty wellingtonia. Rose-lovers will be delighted with the newly restored formal, 1920's rose garden with its symmetrically shaped beds planted in delicate shades of pink and white; the design was drawn for them by the noted rosarian Peter Beales. The grounds are a mix of the formal, informal and wild, with plenty of colour from a series of borders, including the deep herbaceous border which has recently been replanted. Hedges of yew, beech and lime give structure and form, and a copse of decorative trees give shade, good leaf form and colour. Kitchen garden enthusiasts will be envious of the Jerrams' productive and beautifully tended plot, reached via the duck pond – surrounded by masses of flag iris – and the yew hedge walk. On sunny days, linger by the pool garden with its summer house. In spring, enjoy the bulbs in the woodland. A charming family garden.

Rooms:
3 twins, all en suite (bath/shower).
Price:
£35 p.p. Single supp. £10.
Meals:
Dinner, by arrangement, £22.50 p.p. (not Saturday).
Closed:
Christmas & New Year.

From Malmesbury, B4042 towards Wootton Bassett. Approx. 2.5 miles on, fork right to Little Somerford. At bottom of hill, right for Great Somerford. At crossroads, left to Dauntsey. House is 1.25 miles on left on a bend.

Grand and friendly, all at once. You can settle down by the huge fireplace in the handsome panelled drawing room with its log fires in winter, and breakfast or dine in the pink, low-ceilinged dining room with its lovely views of the garden. Caroline's a cordon bleu cook and naturally the scrumptious food includes produce from their wonderful vegetable garden. The guest rooms are light and elegant, the bathrooms pristine. Very much a lived-in family home, with horsey pictures in abundance and a 'rogues' gallery' of family portraits upstairs. Children over 8 welcome.

Idover House

Dauntsey, nr. Chippenham, Wiltshire SN15 4HW

Tel: 01249 720340

Christopher & Caroline Jerram

The Coach House

Upper Wraxall, nr. Bath, Wiltshire SN14 7AG

Tel: 01225 891026 Fax: 01225 892355
venables@compuserve.com

Helga & David Venables

Big, generous beds and sweeping views across the garden, in an ancient hamlet. This is the sort of impeccably managed house that appeals particularly to American visitors and to those who love their comforts: huge main rooms with big windows, lots of flower arrangements with gems from the garden, chintz covered chairs and everything neat, tidy and bright. Bedrooms are smaller with skylights and sloping beam ceilings. Helga can tempt you with croquet, tennis and meals on the lawn in summer.

Map No: 1

THE ELEGANT TWO-ACRE LANDSCAPED GARDEN was created from pastureland 16 years ago. The grounds are 600 feet above sea level, where winter winds whip across the surrounding landscape. Shelter is all-important to protect the more tender plants and the solution has been to design a garden which is a splendid blend of open lawns, well-planted borders and masses of well-placed young trees which create large areas of dappled green. Closely-planted, shaped banks and a natural rockery give further protection and winter interest. The overall mood is one of a private park with both open and intimate areas and plenty of colour. The main lawn is beautifully tended and becomes an excellent croquet lawn in milder weather. Helga is the flower person, David the tree and lawn specialist; they make an excellent team, having brought together a good collection of unusual herbaceous plants and many varieties of shrubs. Helga loves colour theming, and her planting includes a clever mixture of yellows and bronzes in one herbaceous border. Favourite plants include her groups of euphorbias and hostas. There's a delightful ornamental kitchen garden to one side of the house which, like all the garden, has been carefully planned for low maintenance but maximum interest.

Rooms:
1 twin, 1 double and 1 single. Private or shared bathrooms available.
Price:
£25-£30 p.p.
Meals:
Dinner, £12.50-£15 p.p., by arrangement.
Closed:
Never.

From M4 junction 17, west along A420. Turn right to Upper Wraxall. Take first left in village opposite pond. Coach House at end of this private drive.

THE SETTING AND THE WONDERFUL MEDIEVAL architecture of Burghope Manor are everything. It's an historic corner of ancient England hidden by tall walls and steeped in a sense of timelessness. John and Elizabeth have chosen, wisely, to keep garden decoration to a bare minimum and instead developed an elegant parkland which perfectly complements their stunning home; the emphasis is firmly on beautifully maintained lawns set among stands of handsome mature trees. Elizabeth makes one exception to the overall theme of tall hedges, open lawns and canopies of leaves with her much-loved splash of colour by the house itself. This is her narrow, bright border which blossoms with herbaceous perennials like peonies, carpets of annuals and cheery roses. It is deliberately designed to give newcomers a bright and cheerful welcome before they experience the stunning interior of their family home. Sweet-scented honeysuckle clambers over the low entrance and wisteria flowers elegantly on the gabled main frontage with its diamond-like leaded windows. After a day spent visiting some of the many magnificent gardens in the area like Stourhead, Iford Manor, Corsham Court and The Courts, relax in the natural beauty of their restful park. Or simply sit in the little summer house and absorb the grandness of the setting.

Map No: 1

Burghope Manor

Winsley, Bradford-on-Avon, Wiltshire BA15 2LA

Tel: 01225 723557   Fax: 01225 723113
burghope.manor@virgin.net
www.burghopemanor.co.uk

John & Elizabeth Denning

An historic manor house and all that goes with it, plus modern touches where they matter. It looks imposing outside – arched, mullioned windows, jutting gables, tall chimneys – while the interior is, quite breathtakingly, manorial. The vast Tudor fireplace (complete with Elizabethan graffiti), a whole gallery of ancestral oil paintings and the most fascinating historic furniture and artefacts – it's all intriguing. Bedrooms are sunny, luxurious and charming with big beds and views over the grounds.

Rooms:
2 doubles and 1 twin, all en suite (bath/shower).
Price:
£42.50-£50 p.p.
Single supp. £40.
Meals:
For groups only.
Closed:
Christmas & New Year.

A36 Warminster road out of Bath for 5 miles, left onto B3108, under railway bridge and up hill. First right, turn off Winsley bypass into old village, then 1st left, into lane marked 'except for access'.

OPEN, SUNNY AND GENUINE – THAT DESCRIBES Sue and her enclosed, south-facing garden with its distinctive cob walls with tiled roofs. First, artistic Sue restored her home, then turned her attention to developing her informal, one-acre garden. She inherited a backdrop of mature trees and an old fig tree, but precious little else. Over eight years she has indulged her passion for old roses, shrubs like the star-studded Viburnum Plicatum, and plants which climb rampantly; her palette has been subdued colours for the front of the house and the occasional dash of yellow. She adores lavender, too, and has a sweetly-scented lavender path leading from the garden to the house. The grounds, with generous lawns, patios, beds and borders and a playhouse and sandpit for children, slope gently down to a newly created wall border of climbers and herbaceous plants which. A stout new pergola has been added at the centre of this wall border and is now the home of a variety of climbers including clematis and vigorous roses. The kitchen garden, partly screened by a tall, climber-covered wooden fence, provides fruit, veg and herbs for the house. A fascinating garden packed with the charms of youth.

Brickworth Farmhouse

Brickworth Lane, Whiteparish, Salisbury, Wiltshire SP5 2QE

Tel: 01794 884663   Fax: 01794 884186

Sue Barry

What could be more seductive than the smell of home-baked bread wafting out of the kitchen? It sets the scene for this fine George I farmhouse in a quiet spot off the main road, on the edge of the New Forest. The rooms are full of character, ample and charming, with patchwork quilts, brass beds and stencils. Sue Barry is equally characterful and, as a Blue Badge guide, is well-qualified to tell you about the area. Home-made jams, honey and elderflower cordial, and several black Labradors snuffling about.

Rooms:
2 doubles and 1 twin/family room, all en suite; 1 single, private bathroom.
Price:
£24-£26 p.p. Single supp. £10.
Meals:
Available locally.
Closed:
22nd December-3rd January.

From Salisbury A36 towards Southampton. After 5 miles, go down hill towards traffic lights at junction of A36/A37. Turn left 100 yds before this junction. House is on left at top of lane.

The West Wing Abbey Manor

Evesham, Worcestershire WR11 4TB

Tel: 01386 442437
phipps@abbey-manor.fsnet.co.uk

John & Jill Phipps

Enter the West Wing, be greeted by a parade of large medieval gargoyles and figures from Evesham Abbey, and you know this is special. Strong, deep colours complement the scale of the hallway, grand staircase, dining room and drawing room (all open for guests). Wonderful Gothic Revival details everywhere in woodwork and original fittings, some restored by the enthusiastic John and Jill themselves. Bedrooms are sumptuously large, bright and inviting, with pretty floral bed linen and comfortable mattresses... and there's even a billiards room with full-size table.

Map No: 2

JOHN AND JILL DESERVE A MEDAL for the devotion, hard work and inspiration they've employed in the restoration of these 40 acres with their fabulous follies and romantic remains from medieval Evesham Abbey. It was only in 1999 that they made their home in the lofty west wing of this glorious early 19th-century Gothic Revival manor. Of all the residents, they found themselves the elected gardeners and set to work at once. John, a farmer, cleared 20 acres of run-down parkland beset with brambles and put them to pasture. They laboured through the overgrown woodland, rediscovering stone-edged paths and carrying out a cut, burn and re-plant epic which has encouraged countless wild flowers. Jill developed the pretty communal flower garden with rose arches and beds full of interest. Bring wellies in damp weather because you shouldn't miss the full walk around the grounds with its crescendo at the magnificent, five-storey octagonal folly dedicated to Simon de Montfort, who died nearby. Along the way you'll spot monastic relics including abbots' tombs, an extraordinary seat backed by intricate stonework from an abbey window and the huge bases of gothic columns. A small lake is being restored as a place of peace and tranquillity, perfect for an evening glass of wine as you lean back against that medieval stonework. Until recently this was a neglected, uncared for, sleeping beauty. Now it is superb, a hauntingly beautiful 40 acres of woodland, historic relics, mature trees and sweeps of lush grassland.

Rooms:
Family room, 3 single beds, private bathroom;
Family room, 1 double & 1 single, en suite.
Price:
£36 p.p.
Meals:
Dinner, by arrangement.
Closed:
Occasionally.

From Evesham, travel north on A4184, over traffic lights on railway bridge. After 0.7 miles, turn left onto A4538 signed Worcester (The Squires). After 0.4 miles, second entrance on left.

YOU'LL HAVE TO TAKE JUDI'S WORD for it that this immaculately tended garden was a wilderness when she and Steve enthusiastically took on the restoration of their delightful home in 1995. All is utterly transformed indoors and outdoors in their three-quarters of an acre of front and back garden. The front garden lawn is decorated with pretty beds – the back garden is a delight hidden by beech hedges, entered through a rustic rose arch. Here Judi has really gone to town, pursuing her passion for the best plants in a setting surrounded by open countryside. To gain as much space as possible for her plants, she has removed all grass and made a series of large interlocking herbaceous beds and a tapestry of gravel paths. Steve has created height with sturdy pergolas which now are a mass of old fashioned rambling roses and a collection of more than 60 different types of clematis. Judi's other favourite plants include iris and peony which make wonderful displays in late spring. The garden has been designed for texture, colour and form and already her grand designs are coming to fruition. A charming feature is the little water garden which sparkles with water lilies. The mood is informal, the air sweetly scented with fragrant plants. The sort of garden that attracts bees, butterflies, dragonflies, birds and, on open days for the National Gardens Scheme, flocks of garden lovers.

Map No: 2

The Old Vicarage

Darley, Harrogate, Yorkshire HG3 2QF

Tel: 01423 780526   Fax: 01423 780526
judi@darley33.freeserve.co.uk

Judi & Steve Smith

Judi and Steve have lavished care on their sensitive recent restoration of this lovely 1849 vicarage set in the heart of a very pretty village. Balusters and doors have been stripped, old flagstones cleaned, wooden floors cut back, National Trust paints used on walls. The warm, friendly house is full of good china, country furniture, books, even a teddy bear collection. Immaculate bathrooms, one with slipper bath; charming bedrooms, one with a stunning Italian repro brass-and-iron bed. Breakfast in the large dining room overlooking the front garden, relax in comfy sofas in the elegant living room.

Rooms:
1 double, en suite (shower);
1 twin with private bathroom
(bath/shower).
Price:
£25 p.p. Single occ. £30.
Meals:
Dinner, £17.50 p.p.
Closed:
Occasionally.

From Harrogate A59. Turn right for
B6451. Right at Wellington pub.
House is on the right, next to Christ
Church.

ALL FIVE KEYS spent their first year here squeezed into a caravan while building work and landscaping began on a warren of derelict farm buildings. It took two JCBs three weeks to carve out a completely new layout and a further three attempt to achieve the 2.5 acres of landscaping we see today. Annie longed for an informal, sprawling country house garden which would make the most of the views and set off the house; she has succeeded gloriously, adding colour, texture, height and a series of compartments. There were just 15 trees when they began their temporary gypsy lifestyle. Today there are more than 1,500 planted in the garden and their surrounding land where dogs gambol and horses graze. Developed by trial and error over the past 13 years the whole garden has a charmingly organic, natural feel to it, from richly planted herbaceous borders to the new, productive orchard. Old brick and stone has been recycled into walls and steps and a small lake created for the family's beloved East Indian ducks. Sam has built a huge paved pergola as a home for climbing roses and the little summer house is a perfect retreat. Annie's greatest joy, she says, is to watch her lovely trees and plants develop year by year and enjoy seeing their huge efforts blossom into a place of beauty.

Rooms:
1 twin/double, en suite (shower);
1 double/family room, en suite (bath);
1 four-poster with private bathroom.
Price:
From £27 p.p.
Meals:
Dinner, £20 p.p., by arrangement, or good food available at four pubs a short walk away.
Closed:
Occasionally in winter.

From A1(M), take Boroughbridge exit. At North side of Boroughbridge follow Easingwold/Helperby sign. In Helperby, right at T-junction, right up Hall Lane. Left in front of school.

A superbly solid Georgian house with sweeping views across the Vale of York, yet only three minutes walk from the heart of the village. In 28 acres that run down to the River Swale (fishing available), it has black sheep, ducks, horses and ponies, a croquet lawn and a tennis court. The house – largely renovated by the amusing Sam and Annie – is a treat: the large, stylish rooms are all extremely cosy with quirky touches, and the big beamed bedrooms have books, antiques and window seats. One has a four-poster.

Laurel Manor Farm

Brafferton-Helperby, York, Yorkshire YO61 2NZ

Tel: 01423 360436 Fax: 01423 360437 laurelmf@aol.com www.sawdays.co.uk

Sam & Annie Atcherley-Key

Millgate House

Richmond, Yorkshire DL10 4JN

Tel: 01748 823571   Fax: 01748 850701
oztim@millgatehouse.demon.co.uk   www.sawdays.co.uk

Austin Lynch & Tim Culkin

Prepare to be amazed. In every room and in every corner of the garden, the marriage of natural beauty and sophistication exists in a state of bliss. The four Doric columns at the entrance draw you through the hall into the dining room and to views of the Swale Valley. Beds from Heals, period furniture, cast-iron baths, myriad prints and paintings and one double bed so high you wonder how to get onto it. Tim and Austin, both ex-English teachers, have created something very special.

NOTHING OF THE ELEGANT façade of Austin and Tim's home hints at the treasures which lie behind – it makes the shock of discovery even more dramatic. Wandering into the drawing room, you are drawn, magnet-like, to the veranda to discover the full impact of the garden below. A stay at Millgate House without exploring it would be an unforgivable omission; no wonder that when Austin and Tim entered the Royal Horticultural Society's 1995 National Garden Competition, they romped away with first prize from 3,000-plus entries. This famous walled town garden deserves every last bouquet and adulatory magazine and newspaper article it has received. A narrow shady lane to one side of the house, adorned with immaculate hostas, introduces the main garden. Here the long terraced grounds, sloping steeply down towards the river and overlooked by the great Norman castle, are divided into a rhythmic series of lush compartments. All is green, with cascades of foliage breaking out into small, sunny open areas before you dive beneath yet more foliage to explore further secret areas. Plantsmanship, a passion for old roses, hostas, clematis, ferns and small trees and a love of myriad leaf forms come together triumphantly. As William Blake said: "Exuberance is beauty". If you just want to explore the garden you can phone Austin and Tim to arrange a visit.

Rooms:
1 double and 1 twin, both en suite (bath and shower).
1 double with private bathroom and sitting room.
Price:
From £30 p.p. Single supp. £10.
Meals:
Available in Richmond.
Closed:
Never.

Just off Richmond Market Place, house is at bottom of the square opposite side of Barclays Bank. Look for a green door, signed.

Wales

SUE HAS WOVEN A BRILLIANT TAPESTRY into her 750-foot-high hillside garden with breathtaking views across the valley to the Black Mountains. She and Arthur started the garden from scratch in 1986, moving huge quantities of earth, digging two spring-fed ponds, building walls, planting hedges and forming a rockery of massive stones. A professional garden designer and self-confessed plant fanatic, Sue can never resist buying additional treasures for her 2.5 acres of formal, informal and woodland gardens. Each area has been designed and planted with passionate delight, from the welcoming courtyard, with its charming white-arched pergola planted with roses and other climbers, to the steep, woodland avenue which rises to an obelisk at the very top of the garden. On this obelisk is a memorial carving which records that Sue and Arthur made this garden. Wind your way back along twisting paths through woodland planting and a bog garden back to the lower areas with their deep borders and the open patio with beds brimming with colour and interest. The rockery is now mature and a skilful blend of flowers, shrubs and decorative conifers adds height. Around the house, containers of every size explode with a further collection of more tender plants. Every season has its displays with spectacular high points at the beginning of May, the start of July and, in milder years, in September. Garden-lovers flock here from near and far when Sue opens for the National Gardens Scheme… all leave exalted and inspired.

Map No: 1

Great Campston

Llanfihangel Crucorney, Abergavenny
Monmouthshire NP7 8EE

Tel: 01873 890465/890633 Fax: 01873 890766

greatcampston@aol.com
www.gardenloverbreaks.co.uk

Sue & Arthur Gill

History everywhere… beside an old tapestry there is a portrait of Charles I, who dined and stayed here on the 1st July 1645 during the Civil War – he presides over the gnarled and ancient refectory table set for breakfast with flowers and pretty china. Warmly hospitable, Sue has decorated the rooms in strong colours lightening the heavy oak furniture of the dining room. Bedrooms are luxurious and elegant with modern bathrooms/showers. Sue's most surprising touch (apart from her herd of Angora goats) is the Star Bathroom – midnight blue with moons-and-stars wallpaper. In summer, weather permitting, breakfast can be served in the courtyard or conservatory – there's a tennis court too.

Rooms:
1 double, en suite (bath);
2 doubles, 1 twin & 1 single,
all with private bathrooms.
Price:
£25-£35 p.p.
Meals:
Available locally.
Closed:
Never.

M4 to Severn Bridge. At junction 24, right onto A449. 12-13 miles on, exit signed Abergavenny. A40 for 9 miles, then A465 for Hereford. 6 miles on, take right turn marked Grosmont. 2 miles up hill, house is on right.

ARTIST/GARDENER WILLIAM and Philadelphian-born Lynne have designed these delightful four acres – including two acres of walled garden – to make the most of the magnificent landscape which surrounds them. The garden has stunning views of the mighty ruins of Carreg Cennen Castle, the Cennen Valley and the Black Mountains. William is originator of the nearby National Botanic Garden of Wales and the restorer of Aberglasney, (the "garden lost in time"), so you'd expect something very special in his own grounds. Carreg Cennen House gives you just that. The garden is designed to provide a transition from the formal geometry of the house to the natural beauty surrounding it. An arch through the tall beech hedge at the entrance is a tantalising invitation to explore what lies beyond and sinuous mown paths lead through deep grass from one viewpoint to the next. It's almost unbelievable that this largely informal, beautifully planted garden was choked with eight-feet-high brambles when William re-acquired his family home 30 years ago. He and Lynne have transformed a jungle into a series of changing frames, arcs and rectangles with special features including espaliered fruit and a collection of 40 different varieties of fruit tree. The 1806 apiary in the grounds is unique. The best spot to enjoy both garden and the views is from the elegant Regency veranda – from here you can gaze up past a copper beech to the hauntingly atmospheric castle.

Rooms:
2 twins, sharing bathroom.
Price:
£25 p.p.
Meals:
Excellent food available locally.
Closed:
20 December-6 January.

From end of M4, A48 to Cross Hands r'bout. A476 to Llandeilo. From Ffairfach follow signs to Carreg Cennen Castle for 2.5 miles. Turn left into avenue marked by stone walls, just before entering Trap.

Dolls' house Regency architecture with sunny hall, oak floors, tall staircase and perfectly proportioned rooms. Pictures everywhere, including William's garden studies. At the stair head be greeted by a bust of William's ancestor, William Wilkins, architect of the National Gallery. Breakfast in the dining room with its whacky wooden ceiling in red and green, sleep on comfy mattresses in Victorian beds in the cosy white-floored twin, enjoy castle views from the second twin or relax in the little guest sitting room. William and Lynne are delightful hosts, utterly modest movers and shakers in the resurgence of Welsh gardens. Children over 12 welcome.

Carreg Cennen House

Trap, Llandeilo, Carmarthenshire SA19 6TL

Tel: 01558 823242 Fax: 01558 823242

Lynne & William Wilkins

Glynhir Mansion

Llandybie, Ammanford, Carmarthenshire SA18 2TD

Tel: 01269 850438 Fax: 01269 851275
glynhir@glynhir.demon.co.uk
www.sawdays.co.uk

Miss Katy & Mr Julian Jenkins

*The startling shriek of a peacock, clucking of hens and grunts of
contented pot-bellied pigs greet you at this mellow-stoned 1708
mansion at the foot of the Black Mountain in an area of outstanding
natural beauty. Indoors, the large, comfortable sitting room has a
welcoming log fire and a baby grand. Sleep well in one of the four
large bedrooms, wake to comforting farmyard sounds and enjoy the
relaxed, informal atmosphere of Glynhir Mansion. Seize a rare
chance to wallow in the bucolic sights and sounds of a passing
pastoral age.*

Rooms:
2 doubles, en suite
(1 shower, 1 bath),
1 twin with private bathroom.
Self-catering also available.
Price:
From £19.50 p.p. Single supp.
£2 per day peak season.
Check for self-catering prices.
Meals:
Dinner, 3 courses, from
£14 p.p., by arrangement.
Closed:
November-March (except for
large groups).

From M4 to Pont Abraham
services, 2nd exit marked
Llandeilo & Ammanford. There,
left at 2nd set of lights. After 2
miles, right opp. bus shelter and
golf club on left. House is 1 mile
up on right.

KATY WAS AIMING FOR SERENITY when she
began tackling these grounds with their
charming, crumbling dovecote some years ago.
Encroaching rhododendrons around the house
were cut back, banks of nettles and brambles
cleared and lawns created among lovely mature
trees. Today the five-acre grounds – which
include a huge walled garden where fresh veg,
herbs and soft fruit are grown for the house –
achieve all the tranquillity she had hoped for.
The rhododendrons are tamed and flower
energetically, and half an acre has been grassed
over for games, gentle strolls or simply sitting
outside in sunny weather. Lots of perennials are
planted for colour and interest. No wonder art
groups love visiting Glynhir to sketch the
garden and enjoy the views of fields and
mountains. Glynhir's greatest and most
romantic garden treasure, however, is away
from the house and is not to be missed... Take
the walk down woodland along the paths which
the energetic Katy has re-opened to the valley
below. What was a jungle of rampant laurel,
rhododendron and undergrowth has been
transformed into an arcadian woodland above
the River Loughor, where wild flowers which
had lain dormant for decades are thriving once
again. The restored paths lead to an eyrie-like
vantage point with a perfect view of the estate's
spectacular 30-foot waterfall. Katie has even
built a stone seat where you can sit and
contemplate as you watch the roaring cascade.
Dream on...

A LONG, LEAFY, CANOPIED LANE leads to the charmingly informal garden which Freddie has created and cherished in the two acres around her pretty, lime-washed home. It has been hard work. When Freddie moved to Capel Dewi Uchaf from Windsor more than 10 years ago, first she had to tackle the derelict house; then came the garden.

It was overgrown and overshadowed by many shrubs and apple trees which cast the house into deep shade. On the plus side she inherited a mature woodland backdrop, through which a Roman road runs, and tall, sheltering hawthorn hedges to the east. Trees and undergrowth had to be cleared and clinging roots removed before she could start to garden properly. She planned an informal cottage garden with pretty beds of traditional plants and, very important, a substantial vegetable and soft fruit area to supply the house. Little by little, she has achieved what she hoped for with a relaxed blend of lawns, borders and features including a rose-clad pergola and arch. Her vegetable and fruit patch, edged with recycled railway sleepers, is immaculately tended and very productive. One of the most delightful corners is the little front garden with its brightly planted beds which welcome guests to the front door, another the White Garden, a memorial to members of her family. Sit under the pergola and enjoy the richly scented roses, walk the woodland in springtime when bluebells, snowdrops and wood anemones flower, or peep into the adjoining field where wild orchids grow.

Rooms:
1 family suite (2 rooms) and 1 twin, both with private bathrooms;
2 doubles, en suite (bath/shower).
Price:
£25 p.p. Single supp. £12.
Meals:
Packed lunch £6 p.p. Dinner £25 p.p.
Closed:
Christmas.

From Carmarthen take B4300 for about 5 miles to Capel Dewi. Leaving village, follow sign on left and go down the drive off the main road.

Freddie has brought new life to what was a neglected, derelict 14th-century house. She has done a tremendous job by restoring her 'Church of David Higher' in traditional country house style. The house is higher up the river than its sister house in the village (Capel Dewi Isaf, meaning lower) – this is a designated SSSI and you can fish on the private stretch of the water and even have your catch cooked for dinner. You will sink into the comfort of the house – brass beds, patchwork, terracotta walls, beams and fascinating memorabilia in utterly peaceful surroundings.

Map No: 1

Capel Dewi Uchaf Country House

Capel Dewi Road, Capel Dewi, nr. Carmarthen, Carmarthenshire SA32 8AY

Tel: 01267 290799   Fax: 01267 290003   uchaffarm@aol.com

Fredena Burns

The Forest

Kerry, nr. Newtown, Montgomeryshire SY16 4DW

Tel: 01686 626084   Fax: 01686 621438

Jonathan & Veronica Davies

*A fine carved oak staircase makes a real impression in the hallway of
this large, family house. Victorian additions have made this a
wonderfully hospitable and immediately comfortable home. You'll find
light, large rooms, deep cushioned sofas, open fires and luxurious beds.
Lovely French wallpapers set off interesting paintings and traditional
furniture. Veronica is an excellent cook and there's homemade
everything. A devoted bee-keeper, she has five hives in her apiary, so do
ask for her award-winning honey at breakfast.*

Map No: 1

THE SETTING, IN GLORIOUS Montgomeryshire, one of Wales' best-kept secrets, is all important. Hills enfold this three-acre valley garden and everything is in complete harmony with the surrounding countryside. Mature trees, including beech and a flowering Pocket Handkerchief tree, look over the grounds, which were originally laid out in the early 1900s and re-shaped in the 1960s. Extensive replanting was undertaken five years ago by Jonathan and Veronica. Much fresh colour has been added to the herbaceous borders that hug the lush green lawns – one of which is a croquet lawn – and the Davies have indulged their passion for older rose varieties. Other favourites that add extra colour include hostas, which do particularly well here, clematis and penstemons. The large, ancient yew trees mixed with rhododendrons, azaleas and maples help create a soothing and peaceful atmosphere. As Veronica says, with the lyrical sound of the brook running down the secluded valley and the music of constant birdsong, this would have been an ideal retreat for the contemplative Cistercians.

Rooms:
2 doubles and 2 singles,
all with private bathroom.
Price:
£38-£48 p.p.
Meals:
Dinner, £27.50 p.p.
Lunch £12 p.p.
Packed lunch £6 p.p.
Closed:
Christmas & New Year.

B4386 Shrewsbury to Chirbury,
left to Church Stoke on A490,
right to Newtown on A489.
Through Kerry, then left into
Gilfach Lane by bridge. 0.75
miles on, house on left, over
cattle grid after stream.

WHEN IRENE FIRST CAME HERE 17 years ago, she wisely decided to wait for a year to discover which plants she had inherited around her farmhouse home. Twelve months later she had her answer – precious little! So she set to work on her third of an acre of farmyard, determined to make it complement its glorious setting, with wonderful valley views. Hard landscaping began, to create terraces and lawns with flights of steps to give shape and form. The very few worthwhile original features, like the wildlife pond in one corner, were carefully nurtured. In springtime this watery corner is a mass of yellow iris and home to contented newts, toads and frogs. Irene introduced shrubs and climbers including a vigorous jasmine, which now sends a heady scent through the front windows, and planted decorative trees, such as weeping willow. Brick-edged beds are packed with colour and alchemilla mollis encouraged to romp among the gravel patio. There's more colour, too, from scores of pots, hanging baskets and window boxes – Irene is a keen container gardener. The creation of an informal cottage garden was her aim and that is just what she has achieved, raising many annuals herself. Nasturtiums romp, pansies pour from pots, wildflowers spill across steps. The variety and colour are uplifting.

Rooms:
1 double and 1 triple,
both en suite (shower).
Price:
£19.50 p.p. Single occ. £22.
Meals:
Packed lunches, £3 p.p.
Supper available at nearby inn.
Closed:
Never.

A494 east from Ruthin. Left opposite Griffin Hotel onto B5429. After 0.5 miles, right to Llangynhafal. 2 miles on, Esgairlygain is signed on right, 100m past Plas Draw.

Haven't you always dreamed of sleeping in a hayloft? The typical, honey-coloured, former cow byre opposite the 15th-century, wattle-and-daub house has been sensitively converted for guests, keeping its low sloping ceilings, beams and small windows; you can still see the outlines of the original thick stone walls. The easy furniture adds to the relaxed atmosphere, the staircase creaks, the sitting room looks over the Vale of Clwyd and your jolly hosts will drop and collect you from Offa's Dyke walks. Children over 10 welcome.

The Old Barn

Esgairlygain, Llangynhafal, Ruthin, Denbighshire LL15 1RT

Tel: 01824 704047   Fax: 01824 704047

Irene Henderson

Scotland

Auchenskeoch Lodge

By Dalbeattie, Dumfries & Galloway DG5 4PG

Tel: 01387 780277   Fax: 01387 780277

Christopher & Mary Broom-Smith

The Victorian billiard table is full-size, there are lots of books and some fine paintings and sculpture, and the log fires are lit for breakfast. The house is a typical Victorian shooting lodge, built in the 1850s and extended in a pleasantly haphazard style. Christopher is a vintage-car enthusiast; Mary is an excellent cook, using food from their own garden. They are warm hosts and the house feels relaxed, even with a formal sitting room. The bedrooms are large, bright and well-furnished, with good rugs, old long dressing mirrors and the odd chaise longue. Children over 12 welcome.

WOODLAND, A SPARKLING BURN, its very own little fishing loch and heather-covered hills which glow with colour when the ling is in full bloom – the natural beauty surrounding Auchenskeoch Lodge is breathtaking. The climate here is so mild that a fig tree in the grounds produces great quantities of fruit. Christopher and Mary, both keen gardeners, inherited handsome Edwardian bones around the house, set among 20 acres of woods, tall stands of rhododendrons and the sweetest of scents from many azaleas. Mature beech hedges divide the more formal areas near the house into a series of compartments and Christopher and Mary have added several flourishes of their own. They have created a small knot garden by the house, its beds edged by low, manicured box hedges, and built an unusual turf and gravel maze. The large, productive vegetable garden behind the house has an authentic Edwardian period feel. Little box hedges along the path edge the long herbaceous borders and a mass of campanula, marguerites, day lilies and vegetable beds, make an attractive combination of the decorative and the practical. There's an immaculate croquet lawn and paths have been created through the woodland, encouraging gentle strolls into sublime countryside.

Rooms:
3 twins/doubles, all en suite (bath/shower).
Price:
£29-£32 p.p. Single occ. £38.
Meals:
Dinner, £17.50 p.p., available on request. Packed lunch from £3.50 p.p.
Closed:
November-Easter.

From Dalbeattie, south-east on B793. Auchenskeoch is 7 miles down this road on right. Turn right and, after 30 yards, left through gate posts.

Nether Underwood

By Symington, Kilmarnock, Ayrshire KA1 5NG

Tel: 01563 830666   Fax: 01563 830777

netherund@aol.com   www.netherunderwood.co.uk

Felicity & Austin Thomson

Map No: 4

Felicity is a very keen gardener and she relished the huge challenge of these grounds when she and Austin moved here 10 years ago. They inherited wonderful 'bones' with an 18th-century, two-acre walled garden and a further 13 acres of woodland and fields with sweeping views. The downside was that the garden, which had once been the kitchen garden for the nearby manor, had been abandoned for years and had reverted to a jungle. Two years of relentless work followed – clearance, weed control and rescue work on hedges and neglected plants. The stranger, most interesting specimens were dug out, fed and re-planted with masses of mulching. The Thomsons called in a landscape gardener for advice on an overall design and began to breathe new life into the grounds; lawns were rejuvenated, new borders laid out, the rose garden nurtured back to colourful splendour. Lots of ornamental planting was introduced to add all-year interest, with good shrubs and trees. An avenue of pleached lime has been planted as well as other formal features including low box hedges as edgings. A kitchen garden has been established for soft fruit, vegetables and cut flowers for the house. One of the garden's greatest bonuses is the stream; it runs though the garden and into the woodland beyond and the banks are home to ducks and water-loving plants and ducks. The sleeping beauty has awoken and matured into a charming example of informal gardening in a natural setting.

You'll quickly feel at home in this unusual, elegantly decorated 1930s-style home built by the original owners of the nearby big house. The large yellow drawing room with Adam fireplace is a replica of the one in their previous home. Felicity serves delicious food at the refectory table in the dark red dining room – she is a former chef who specialises in Scottish fare and home baking. Antique furniture, rich, thick curtains, lovely cosy bedrooms – the twin has tartan and thistle motifs. Colour everywhere and, in the background, the gentle tick-tock of Austin's collection of longcase clocks.

Rooms:
3 doubles, en suite (bath/shower); 1 twin with private bathroom.
Price:
£40 p.p. Single supp. £10.
Meals:
High tea (£5 p.p.) and dinner available.
Closed:
Occasionally.

From Kilmarnock, south on A77, and take first left after Hansel village, signed Underwood and Ladykirk. Left at next 2 junctions, then left into lane 20yds after entrance to Underwood House. House is near the end on the left.

Home Farm

Stobo, Peebles, Peeblesshire EH45 8NX

Tel: 01721 760245   Fax: 01721 760319
hugh.seymour@btinternet.com

Hugh & Georgina Seymour

A turreted entrance makes quite an impression as you arrive at this traditional Peebleshire farmhouse – the old factor's house on the Stobo estate. Built around a courtyard, Hugh and Georgina's home is a place of oak floors, mahogany furniture, attractive pictures and log fires. From the windows you glimpse the large collection of different roses. Bedrooms on the first floor are light and airy and have bathrooms en suite: there is also an attic twin bedded spare room with adjoining bathroom. For those who prefer their own space, there's a cosy self-contained cottage in the outer courtyard.

Map No: 3

AT THE SEYMOURS' HOME you can explore two utterly contrasting gardens: their own plant and shrub filled garden around the house divided into 'rooms' – orchard, kitchen garden, rose garden – and then, though a gate in one corner, the magic of the famous Stobo Castle Japanese Water Garden. The castle, now a health spa, originally belonged to the family but the Seymours have kept up the connection by maintaining the Water Garden as well as their own garden next door. Stobo Water Garden is a rare example of Japanese influenced design in Scotland, originally laid out nearly 100 years ago. Imaginative planting is as much a feature as the visual impact – not to mention the sound – of rushing clear water. There is a dramatic waterfall, and plenty of rills and mini cascades. The water is forged by frequent stepping stones, inviting visitors to criss-cross from one bank to the other. Azaleas and rhododendrons, and many fine specimen trees, are at their finest in May and June, and again in October. The view of the humpback bridge, probably the focal point of the garden, has been much photographed and will be familier to many who have not been within miles of Stobo.

Rooms:
1 twin, en suite, with adjacent dressing room with single bed; 1 twin/double with private bathroom; 1 twin with adjoining bathroom.
Price:
£30 p.p. Single supp. £10. Cottage, let by the week, by arrangement.
Meals:
Dinner, by arrangement, from £20 p.p.
Closed:
Occasionally.

From A72 Peebles/Glasgow, take B712. Turn right down Stobo Castle Health Spa drive then right before small bridge, over cattle grid and up hill, leaving corn mill on left, keep left into courtyard at top.

Public gardens to visit

Some gardens to visit

You'll doubtless have your own national garden guides on your journeys around Britain - and you'll have the added benefit of advice from each of our owners on the best gardens, large and small, in their part of the world. Listen to them - you might find a little-known treasure which you will recall with pleasure for years to come.

Our owners can tell you if one or more of their favourite private gardens are holding open days at the time of your visit and point you in the right direction. These private gardens, many of which open to raise money for the praiseworthy National Gardens Scheme charity, are often the most enjoyable of all. They are highly individual creations with many personal touches created by inspired amateur gardeners who are often on hand to chat to visitors. It's always useful to have a copy of the latest edition of the annual Yellow Book, the National Garden Scheme's *Gardens Of England & Wales Open For Charity*, or Scotland's Gardens Scheme handbook: *Gardens Of Scotland*.

Britain is so rich in famous gardens that we thought an aide-memoire to some of the best might be useful. It is a daunting task to choose favourites from such a wealth of masterpieces and we apologise for any omissions.

Do check the opening times before you make a special journey. We have given all the telephone numbers.

NT = National Trust

NTS = National Trust of Scotland

Public gardens to visit

South West

Tresco Abbey, Isles of Scilly.
Tel: 01720 424105

The semi-tropical plantsman's paradise begun in the 1830s and now in exotic maturity. Just a helicopter ride away from Penzance.

Lost Gardens of Heligan, Pentewan, nr. Mevagissey, Cornwall.
Tel: 01726 844157

Europe's largest garden reconstruction project with restored Italian and Japanese gardens, greenhouse and summer houses.

Rosemoor, Great Torrington, Devon.
Tel: 01805 624067

Lady Anne Palmer's creation, now run by the Royal Horticultural Society. New gardens being developed with generous borders, formal rose and colour-themed gardens.

Knightshayes Court (NT), Bolham, nr. Tiverton, Devon.
Tel: 01884 254665

Woodland walks with many rare trees, formal terraces, witty topiary, formal pool garden.

Barrington Court (NT), nr. Ilminster, Somerset.
Tel: 01460 241938

One of Gertrude Jekyll's final commissions, with three garden rooms including the stunning iris garden.

Hadspen Garden, Castle Cary, Somerset.
Tel: 01749 813707

Large, beautifully planted garden made by Margaret Hobhouse in the early 20th century, restored by Penelope Hobhouse in the 1970s and now run by outstanding colourists/plantsmen Nori & Sandra Pope.

Hestercombe House, Cheddon Fitzpaine, nr. Taunton, Somerset.
Tel: 01823 337222

Two outstanding gardens-within-a-garden, the glorious Lutyens/Jekyll creation by the house and the Georgian landscape garden now being restored by Somerset County Council.

Public gardens to visit

Tintinhull House Garden (NT), Tintinhull, nr. Yeovil, Somerset.
Tel: 01935 822545

One of Somerset's loveliest, a 1930s masterpiece created by Phyllis Reiss with a series of garden rooms each with a distinctive and triumphant character of its own.

Athelhampton House, nr. Dorchester, Dorset.
Tel: 01305 848363

Perfectionist 1890 garden designed by F. Inigo Thomas. Giant yew pyramids, balustrades, narrow canal and eight walled gardens.

Bowood House, nr. Calne, Wiltshire.
Tel: 01249 812102

Grand, elegant landscape garden, the work of Capability Brown and Humphrey Repton. Italianate terraces, rhododendron walks, follies.

Iford Manor, nr. Bradford-on-Avon, Wiltshire.
Tel: 01225 862364

The great architect/garden designer Harold Peto's Edwardian masterpiece. Terraces, classical statuary and architectural relics on a wooded hillside setting.

Stourhead (NT), Stourton, nr. Warminster, Wiltshire.
Tel: 01747 841348

England's best-known landscape garden and one of the most famous of all. Created by banker Henry Hoare in the 1740s, a dream world of follies and walks around a serene lake.

Public gardens to visit

 ## South and South East

Royal Botanic Gardens, Kew, Richmond, Surrey.
Tel: 0208 332 5000
Brilliant plants everywhere in the landscaped gardens and huge
conservatories, with the awe-inspiring Chinese pagoda soaring above you
and a stunning Thames-side setting, too.

Syon Park and Gardens, Brentford, Middlesex.
Tel: 0208 560 0881
Superb country house by Robert Adam, one of Britain's finest
conservatories, glorious collection of trees, long narrow lake. Could central
London really be so close?

Hampton Court, East Molesey, Surrey.
Tel: 0208 781 9500
Beautifully tended gardens around one of Britain's most historic houses
with gems including the knot garden, utterly bewildering yew maze, privy
and sunken pond gardens, topiary, lime avenues.

The Sir Harold Hillier Garden and Arboretum, Romsey, Hamsphire.
Tel: 01794 368787
The national collection of oaks and one of the largest collection of plants in
Britain - famed for its acid-lovers.

Mottisfont Abbey Garden (NT), nr. Romsey, Hamsphire.
Tel: 01794 340757
A place of pilgrimage for rose-lovers who come to delight in the National
Collection of pre-1900 shrub roses set in a beautifully designed garden.

Denmans, Fontwell, Sussex.
Tel: 01243 542808
The home of celebrated garden designer/writer John Brookes' School of
Garden Design... a gem from the moment you enter through the
enormous glasshouse.

Leonardslee Gardens, Lower Beeding, nr. Horsham, Sussex.
Tel: 01403 891212
The famous Loder family woodland garden - rhododendrons were their
great passion, as you'll discover.

Public gardens to visit

Nymans (NT), Handscross, nr. Haywards Heath, Sussex.
Tel: 01444 400321

It's more than a century since Leonard Messel began to make this ravishing garden with its wealth of acid-lovers in a hauntingly romantic setting.

Wakehurst Place Gardens (NT), nr. Ardingly, Haywards Heath, Sussex.
Tel: 01444 894049

The Royal Botanical Society's beautifully planted home in the South with magnificent trees and shrubs - the Himalayan Glade is stunning.

Great Dixter, Northiam, nr. Rye, Sussex.
Tel: 01797 253107

Originally laid out by Edwin Lutyens and now beautifully developed by distinguished gardener and garden writer Christopher Lloyd. Always changing, always inspiring.

Bateman's (NT), Burwash, nr. Etchingham, Sussex.
Tel: 01435 882302

Rudyard Kipling's 17th-century home for more than 30 years. Much of the garden was designed by the great writer: rose garden, old yew hedges, long pool, double pleached lime walk.

Sissinghurst Garden (NT), nr. Cranbrook, Kent.
Tel: 01580 715330

The world-famous masterpiece created from the 1930s onwards by Vita Sackville-West and Harold Nicolson. Rose Garden, Cottage Garden, White Garden - all are classics.

Penshurst Place, nr. Tonbridge, Kent.
Tel: 01892 870307

14th-century house and one of England's most historic gardens, divided into a series of wonderfully-planted compartments.

Hever Castle, nr. Edenbridge, Kent.
Tel: 01732 865224

Superb Italianate garden with classical statuary collected by William Waldorf Astor, all created around a moated castle.

Public gardens to visit

Wisley Garden, Wisley, nr. Ripley, Woking, Surrey.
Tel: 01483 224234
The Royal Horticultural Society's Surrey home is a place of pilgrimage for garden-lovers from across the world. Glorious at any time of year.

The Gardens Of The Rose, Chiswell Green, St Albans, Hertfordshire.
Tel: 01727 850461
Rosarians will be in heaven - more than 2,000 varieties thrive at the Royal National Rose Society's headquarters.

Hatfield House, Hatfield, Hertfordshire.
Tel: 01707 262823
Richly historic house and garden brilliantly restored over the past 30 years in a superb recreation of stately English country house gardening at its loveliest.

Stowe Gardens (NT), nr. Buckingham.
Tel: 01280 822850
Epic Georgian landscape garden with buildings by Vanbrugh, Gibbs and Kent with arches, temples, Palladian bridge and other monuments in sweeping lakeside setting.

Public gardens to visit

 ## Cotswolds/Midlands

Sudeley Castle, Winchcombe, Gloucestershire.
Tel: 01242 602308

The gardens-within-a-garden around the spell-binding castle become more beautiful with time, thanks to a team effort by inspired designers including Rosemary Verey.

Kiftsgate Court, nr. Chipping Campden, Gloucestershire.
Tel: 01386 438777

June is sensational at Kiftsgate, when the roses and borders are at their best, but spring and autumn have their delights in this ravishingly artistic garden.

Hidcote Manor Garden (NT), nr. Chipping Campden,
Gloucestershire. Tel: 01386 438333

One of the quintessential English country gardens, a masterpiece of design, a triumph of early 20th-century bravura. And Kiftsgate is only a few steps away.

Barnsley House, Barnsley, nr. Cirencester, Gloucestershire.
Tel: 01285 740281

Rosemary Verey's breathtaking, superbly designed, beautifully worked and bountifully planted Englishwoman's garden with the most photographed laburnum walk in the country.

Painswick Rococo Garden, Painswick, Gloucestershire.
Tel: 01452 813204

Step back in time to enjoy this lovingly restored formal 18th-century garden of avenues and follies, water and geometric designs. The early spring snowdrop displays are famous.

Rodmarton Manor, Rodmarton, nr. Tetbury, Gloucestershire.
Tel: 01285 841253

Glorious Cotswolds garden created around a fine Arts and Crafts manor. Beautifully planted compartments, hedges, dry stone walls and a superb hornbeam avenue set in woodland.

Westonbirt Arboretum, nr. Tetbury, Gloucestershire.
Tel: 01666 880220

Crowds come in Autumn to enjoy one of the finest leaf colour displays in England, but there is year-round interest all year.

Public gardens to visit

Stone House Cottage, nr. Kidderminster, Worcestershire.
Tel: 01562 69902
A fantasy of brick-built follies, lavish planting and fine plants set within an
old walled kitchen garden.

 ## East Anglia

The Beth Chatto Gardens, Elmstead Market, nr. Colchester, Essex.
Tel: 01206 822007
Gardening in extremis. Famed plantswoman Beth Chatto has transformed a
boggy field surrounded by unpromising dry areas into magnificent displays.
Specialist nursery with heaps of unusual plants.

Melford Hall (NT), nr. Sudbury, Suffolk.
Tel: 01787 880286
The star attraction is the glorious octagonal gazebo, dominating a garden
with lawns, topiary and a dry moat developed as a sunken garden.

Helmingham Hall, nr. Stowmarket, Suffolk.
Tel: 01473 890363
Beautiful country house garden which perfectly complements the lovely old
house. Box-edged parterre, wide, luscious borders, the sweetest scented
roses, a Tudor garden and much, much more.

Blickling Hall (NT), Aylsham, Norfolk.
Tel: 01263 733084
Very fine Jacobean house with handsome formal garden including parterre
of square herbaceous beds, Doric temple, orangery and parkland.

Public gardens to visit

 ## The North

Bridgemere Garden World, nr. Nantwich, Cheshire.
Tel: 01270 520381

A garden centre which is a plant-lovers' paradise set in 25 acres, including a three-acre display garden to show off some of the countless plants available.

Little Moreton Hall (NT), nr. Congleton, Cheshire.
Tel: 01260 272018

One of the best half-timbered houses, complete with moat. Many medieval plants, box hedges and yew topiary.

Biddulph Grange Garden (NT), nr. Congleton, Cheshire.
Tel: 01782 517999

The National Trust's masterly restoration of a fine early-Victorian garden full of exciting exotic touches like dragons and other oriental features and named areas devoted to plants from countries including China and Egypt.

Hardwick Hall (NT), nr. Chesterfield, Derbyshire.
Tel: 01246 850430

Bess of Hardwick's late 16th-century home adorned with grand gardens laid out in the early 20th century in Elizabethan stoned courts. The herb garden is the largest and most impressive in England.

Castle Howard, nr. Malton, North Yorkshire.
Tel: 01653 648444

Riotously extravagant formal park designed by Vanbrugh and Hawksmoor around palatial Castle Howard. Huge avenues, lake, temples, awe-inspiring fountain and lovely rose garden.

Harlow Carr Botanical Gardens, Harrogate, North Yorkshire.
Tel: 01423 565418

Harlow Carr is to the North what Wisley is to the South. Set in a gentle valley, it's a showcase for the best plants which thrive in the region.

Newby Hall Gardens, Ripon, North Yorkshire.
Tel: 01423 322583

Supremely designerly garden with strong influences from Hidcote. A series of gardens-within-a-garden, statue walk and tropical, rock and woodland gardens.

Public gardens to visit

Holker Hall, nr. Grange-over-Sands, Cumbria.
Tel: 01539 558328

Fine formal garden by the house, yew hedges, gravel walks, large walled garden, arboretum and meadow garden, all set around the handsome house rebuilt in the late 19th century after a fire.

Levens Hall, nr. Kendal, Cumbria.
Tel: 01539 560321

A magnet for those who love topiary at its most flamboyant, with absolutely masses of dizzily shaped box and yew in the form of figures, chess pieces etc. Lots more, too, including lovely rose garden.

Public gardens to visit

 Wales

**National Botanic Garden of Wales, Middleton Hall,
Llanarthne, Carmarthenshire.
Tel: 01558 667132/4**
Newly opened, this world of plants has an entire Mediterranean landscape
within the world's largest single span glasshouse and one of Europe's
longest herbaceous borders, all set in an immaculately restored Regency
park.

**Aberglasney, Llangathen, Carmarthenshire.
Tel: 01558 668998**
The 'garden lost in time', a rare survival of a 16th/17th-century garden
now, after decades of neglect and vandalism, undergoing a brilliant
restoration programme which looks set to make it one of Britain's finest.

**Powis Castle (NT), Welshpool, Powys.
Tel: 01938 554338**
Truly historic garden with magnificent late 17th-century terraces, glorious
borders, gigantic yews, sweeping lawns and small woodland garden.

**Chirk Castle (NT), Chirk, nr. Oswestry, County Wrexham.
Tel: 01691 777701**
Massive 13th-century border castle guarded by huge yew hedges and
topiary, with lawns and a woodland garden with magnolias and
rhododendrons.

**Plas Newydd (NT), Llanfairpwll, Anglesey, Gwynedd.
Tel: 01248 714795**
Late 18th-century gothic fantasy above the Menai Straits, with small,
attractive terraced garden and wonderful parkland with lovely ornamental
trees.

**Bodnant (NT), nr. Colwyn Bay, Conway.
Tel: 01492 650460**
Sheltered in its valley, a little bit of the Himalayas in Wales with
rhododendrons and camellias galore. Formal features include wonderful
laburnum tunnel, Italian terrace, ponds, yew hedges.

Public gardens to visit

 ## Scotland

Logan Botanic Garden, Port Logan, Dumfries and Galloway.
Tel: 01776 860231

Specialist garden with grand tree ferns, cabbage palms and many rare, unusual and interesting plants from the southern hemisphere.

Royal Botanic Gardens, Inverleith Row, Arboretum Place, Edinburgh.
Tel: 0131 552717

Exotic plants galore in the Glasshouse Experience, outstanding rock garden and one of the largest collections of rhododendrons in the world.

Glasgow Botanic Gardens, Great Western Road, Glasgow.
Tel: 0141 3342422

Founded in 1817 by Tomas Hopkirk around the Kibble Palace. Large collection of orchids, ferns and begonias within the main glasshouses.

Arduaine Garden (NTS), Kilmelford, nr. Oban.
Tel: 01852 200366

Spectacular garden renowned for its collection of rhododendrons, azaleas, magnolias and fine herbaceous perennials.

Crathes Castle and Walled Garden (NTS), nr. Banchory, Grampian.
Tel: 01330 844525

Strong Hidcote influences in the large walled garden which has eight separate areas including herbaceous borders brimming with unusual plants. The great yew hedge is 300 years old.

Quick reference indices

WHEELCHAIR

These owners have told us that they have facilities suitable for people in wheelchairs. It is essential that you confirm on the telephone what is available before arrival.

England

56 • 69

Scotland

97

ACCESS

These houses have bedrooms or bathrooms that are accessible for people of limited mobility. Please phone beforehand to confirm details and special needs.

England

6 • 9 • 11 • 15 • 21 • 29 • 30 • 35 • 43 • 58 • 61 • 65 • 69 • 75 • 80

Wales

91 • 95

GOOD FOR SINGLES

These are B&Bs which have single rooms, or which do not charge a single supplement.

England

19 • 20 • 23 • 24 • 48 • 50 • 64 • 65 • 67 • 68 • 70 • 72 • 84 • 86 • 87

Wales

91 • 95

CHILD-FRIENDLY

The owners of these houses welcome children of any age, but it is best to phone beforehand to discuss any special needs. Cots and highchairs may not be available.

England

1 • 5 • 6 • 7 • 10 • 11 • 13 • 15 • 19 • 20 • 23 • 24 • 27 • 30 • 32 • 34 • 35 • 41 • 44 • 46 • 48 • 54 • 58 • 63 • 64 • 65 • 67 • 69 • 70 • 72 • 74 • 77 • 78 • 80 • 81 • 86 • 89

Wales

91 • 93 • 94 • 95 • 96

Scotland

97 • 99

EVENING MEALS

These B&Bs offer evening meals.

England

1 • 2 • 4 • 5 • 8 • 9 • 10 • 13 • 14 • 15 • 16 • 17 • 20 • 22 • 23 • 27 • 30 • 31 • 33 • 35 • 36 • 40 • 41 • 42 • 43 • 44 • 46 • 50 • 52 • 55 • 57 • 59 • 63 • 64 • 68 • 69 • 71 • 72 • 73 • 80 • 81 • 83 • 84 • 88 • 89

Wales

93 • 94 • 95 • 96 • 97

Scotland

99

Quick reference indices

GROWN

These owners use mostly organic ingredients, chemical-free, home-grown or locally-grown produce.

England

1 • 4 • 6 • 8 • 12 • 14 • 15 • 16 • 18 • 19 • 20 • 21 • 22 • 23 • 28 • 34 • 38 • 42 • 43 • 44 • 46 • 49 • 51 • 56 • 57 • 58 • 59 • 61 • 63 • 65 • 67 • 68 • 70 • 76 • 78 • 80 • 81 • 83 • 86 • 88

Wales

94 • 95

Scotland

98

PETS WELCOME

The owners of these houses are happy to discuss the idea of your bringing your prize pet on holiday.

England

5 • 6 • 11 • 17 • 20 • 23 • 30 • 35 • 39 • 41 • 44 • 58 • 63 • 64 • 69 • 70 • 72 • 77 • 80 • 89 • 90

Wales

95 • 96

Scotland

97

LICENSED

These B&Bs are licensed.

England

4 • 11 • 13 • 15 • 30 • 32 • 35 • 42 • 43 • 55 • 56 • 60 • 68 • 69 • 71 • 73 • 83 • 89

Wales

93 • 94 • 95

Scotland

97

Alastair Sawday
Special Places to Stay series

Tel: 01275 464891 Fax: 01275 464887
www.sawdays.co.uk

Order Form UK

All these books are available in major bookshops or you may order them direct. Post and packaging are FREE.

	Price	No. copies
***Special Places to Stay:* French Bed & Breakfast** Edition 6	£13.95	
***Special Places to Stay:* British Hotels, Inns and other places** Edition 2	£10.95	
***Special Places to Stay:* British Bed & Breakfast** Edition 5	£12.95	
***Special Places to Stay:* French Hotels, Inns and other places** Edition 1	£11.95	
***Special Places to Stay:* Italy (from Rome to the Alps)** Edition 1	£9.95	
Special Places to Stay in Spain & Portugal Edition 3	£11.95	
Special Places to Stay in Ireland Edition 2	£10.95	
***Special Places to Stay:* Paris Hotels** Edition 2	£8.95	
The Little Earth Book	£4.99	
Please make cheques payable to: **Alastair Sawday Publishing** **Total**		

Please send cheques to: Alastair Sawday Publishing, The Home Farm, Barrow Gurney, Bristol BS48 3RW. **For credit card orders call 01275 464891 or order directly from our website www.sawdays.co.uk**

Name:

Address:

Postcode:

Tel: Fax:

If you do not wish to receive mail from other companies, please tick the box ☐

GBB1

Order Form USA

All these books are available at your local bookstore, or you may order direct. Allow two to three weeks for delivery.

Special Places to Stay: **British Hotels, Inns** and other places

	Price	No. copies
Edition 2	$14.95	

Special Places to Stay: **British Bed & Breakfast**

Edition 5	$19.95	

Special Places to Stay: **French Hotels, Inns** and other places

Edition 1	$19.95	

Special Places to Stay: **French Bed & Breakfast**

Edition 6	$19.95	

Special Places to Stay: **Paris Hotels**

Edition 2	$14.95	

Special Places to Stay in Ireland

Edition 2	$19.95	

Special Places to Stay in Spain & Portugal

Edition 3	$19.95	

Special Places to Stay: **Italy (from Rome to the Alps)**

Edition 1	$14.95	

Shipping in the continental USA: $3.95 for one book, $4.95 for two books, $5.95 for three or more books. Outside continental USA, call (800) 243-0495 for prices. For delivery to AK, CA, CO, CT, FL, GA, IL, IN, KS, MI, MN, MO, NE, NM, NC, OK, SC, TN, TX, VA, and WA, please add appropriate sales tax

Please make checks payable to: The Globe Pequot Press   **Total**

To order by phone with MasterCard or Visa: (800) 243-0495. 9 a.m. to 5 p.m. EST; by fax: (800) 820-2329, 24 hours; through our Website: www.globe-pequot.com; or by mail: The Globe Pequot Press, P.O. Box 480, Guilford, CT 06437.

Name: Date:

Address:

Town:

State: Zip code:

Tel: Fax:

GBB1

The Little Earth Book

The Little Earth Book

Alastair Sawday, the publisher of this (wonderful) guidebook, is also an environmentalist. For over 25 years he has campaigned, not only against the worst excesses of modern tourism and its hotels, but against environmental 'looniness' of other kinds. He has fought for systems and policies that might enable our beautiful planet - simply - to survive. He founded and ran Avon Friends of the Earth, has run for Parliament, and has led numerous local campaigns. He is now a trustee of the Soil Association, experience upon which he draws in this remarkable new book.

Researched and written by an eminent Bristol architect, James Bruges, *The Little Earth Book* is a clarion call to action, a mind-boggling collection of mini-essays on today's most important environmental concerns, from global warming and poisoned food to economic growth, Third World debt, genes and 'superbugs'. Undogmatic but sure-footed, the style is light, explaining complex issues with easy language, illustrations and cartoons. Ideas are developed chapter by chapter, yet each one stands alone. It is an easy browse.

The Little Earth Book provides hope, with new ideas and examples of people swimming against the current, of bold ideas that work in practice. It is a book as important as it is original. One has been sent to every M.P. Now you, too, can learn about the issues and join the most important debate of this century.

Oh - one last thing: *The Little Earth Book* is a damned good read! Note what Jonathon Porritt says about it:

"The Little Earth Book is different. And instructive. And even fun."

Did you know.....

- If everyone adopted the Western lifestyle we would need five earths to support us

- 60% of infections picked up in hospitals are now drug-resistant

- Environmental diasters have already created 80 MILLION refugees

Report Form

Comments on existing entries and new discoveries.

If you have any comments on entries in this guide, please let us have them.
If you have a favourite house, hotel, inn or other new discovery, please let
us know about it.

Report on:

Entry no: Edition:

New recommendation:

Name of property:

Address:

                                       Postcode:

Tel:

Comments:

From:

Address:

                                       Postcode:

Tel:

Please send the completed form to: **Alastair Sawday Publishing,
The Home Farm, Barrow Gurney, Bristol BS48 3RW, UK**

Thank you.

GBB1

Turf labyrinth, Morville, Shropshire, designed by Kathy Swift and photographed by Andrew Lawson

The National Gardens Scheme
Gardens Open For Charity

Garden gates swing open to the public every year for charity, allowing visitors in to see what is behind the hedges of some of the finest private gardens in England and Wales.

Innovative or classic, the NGS embraces them all, from intimate city courtyards and cottage plots to 18th Century landscapes. Find novel solutions to all kinds of garden problems and enjoy privileged insight into inventive planting schemes. Interesting and unusual plants are often available, along with expert tips from the people in the know.

Gardens of England and Wales Open For Charity, the best-selling annual guide published by the NGS, lists all open days with short descriptions of the gardens. The 'Yellow Book', as it is familiarly known, is available at all major booksellers, and is also available on the NGS website.

Garden Finder, a search and mapping facility on the NGS website provides even more information about the gardens, often including photographs. Plan your itinerary using the latest opening information, including some garden openings exclusively announced on the NGS website **www.ngs.org.uk**

If you would like more information, or are interested in finding out about opening your own garden for the Scheme please contact:

Catherine Stepney, Public Relations Administrator
The National Gardens Scheme, Hatchlands Park, East Clandon, Surrey GU4 7RT

T 01483 211535   F 01483 211537   E ngs@ngs.org.uk

The Royal Horticultural Society

inspiration fo
all gardener:

For gardening advice, ideas and inspiration, join the RHS and take advantage of almost 200 years of expertise.

Membership benefits to be enjoyed all year:

- Free Gardening Advice Service from the RHS expe:
- Free access with a guest to RHS Gardens Wisley, Rosemoor and Hyde Hall
- Free access to a further 58 gardens across Britain
- Free monthly copy of *The Garden* magazine
- Free Newsletters with details on Members' discour to local talks, tours and demonstrations
- Privileged entry and discounted tickets to 19 Flowe Shows, including Chelsea, Hampton Court Palace and Tatton Park

Let the RHS help you make the most of your gardening year for just £36 (£29, including a one-off £7 joining fee) or SAVE £7 when you join by direct debit and pay just £29.

To join, simply call RHS Membership
Enquiries on: **020 7821 3000**

Lines are open 9am-5.30pm, Monday to Friday. (please quote code 169

Subscription rate valid until 31 October 2001

Registered charity no. 222879 **www.rhs.org.uk**

THE ROYAL
HORTICULTURAL
SOCIETY

Photograph by Sue Snell, *Tulipa* 'Spring Green'

Index by surname

Index by surname

Index by surname

Index by place name

Index by place name

Index by place name

Exchange rate table

£sterling	US$
1	1.49
5	7.45
7	10.43
10	14.90
15	22.35
17	25.33
20	29.80
25	37.25
30	44.70
35	52.15
40	59.60
45	67.05
50	74.50

US$	£sterling
1	0.67
5	3.35
7	4.69
10	6.70
15	10.05
20	13.40
25	16.75

Rates correct at time of going to press September 2000

Symbols

Symbols

Treat each one as a guide rather than a statement of fact and check important points when booking:

 Working farm.

 Children of all ages are positively welcomed but cots, highchairs, etc are not necessarily available.

 Pets are welcome but may have to sleep in an outbuilding or in your car. There may be a supplement to pay or size restrictions.

 Vegetarians catered for with advance warning.

 Most, but not necessarily all, ingredients are organic, organically grown, home-grown or locally grown.

 Full wheelchair facilities for at least one bedroom and bathroom and access to ground-floor common areas.

 Basic ground-floor access for people of limited mobility and at least one bedroom accessible without steps.

 No smoking anywhere in the house.

 This house has pets of its own in the house: dog, cat, parrot...

 Credit cards accepted; most commonly Visa and MasterCard.

 The premises are licensed..